The Video Nasty Colouring Book

By

Tony Newton & Kerry Newton

Recreate those grindhouse, sleaze filled video nasty posters of yesteryear with this fun packed adult colouring book!

Each poster is on its own single sided page ideal to frame or display.

You will need a ruler, fine liner and colouring pens/pencils to recreate your own video nasty posters.

The book they tried to ban!

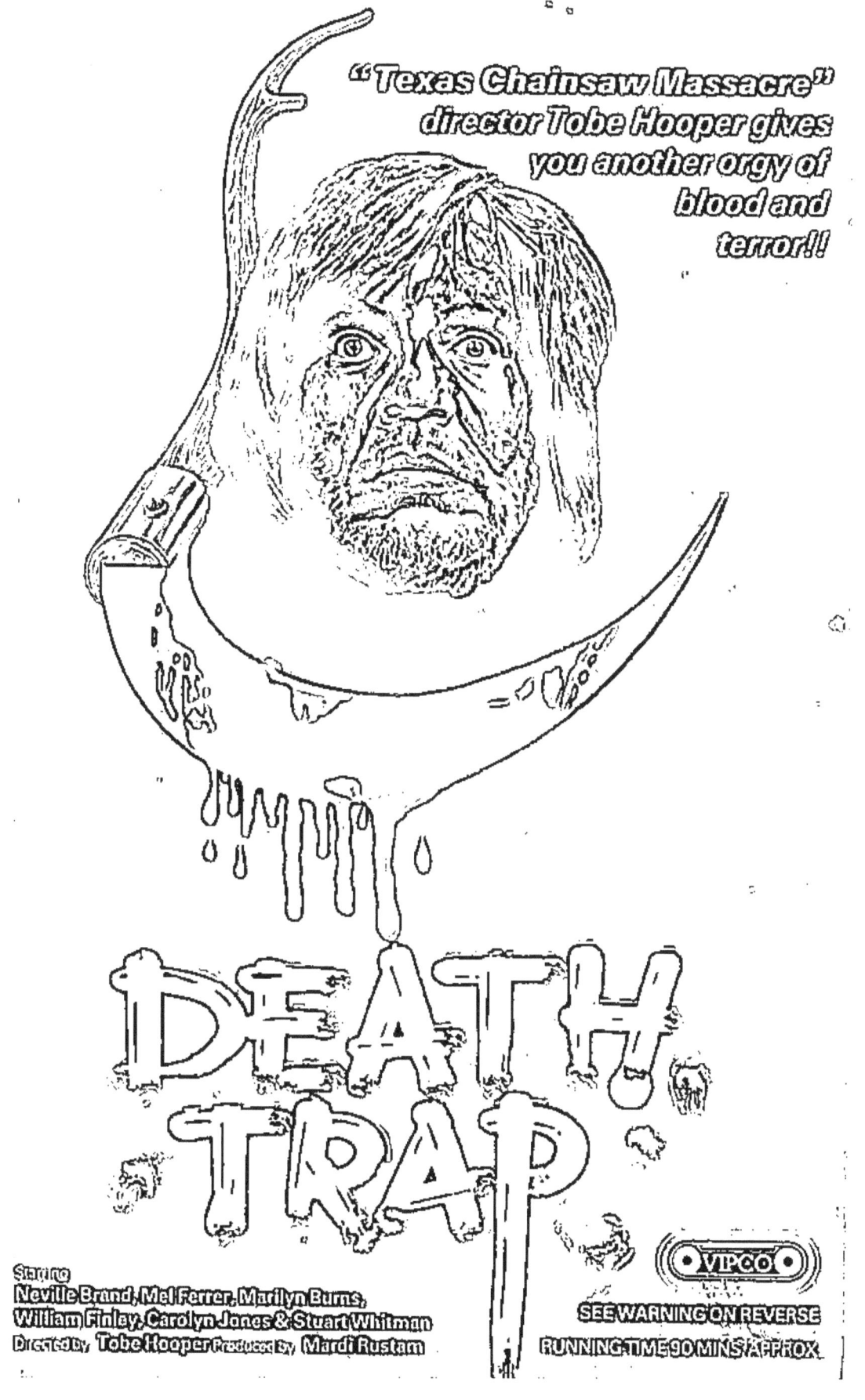

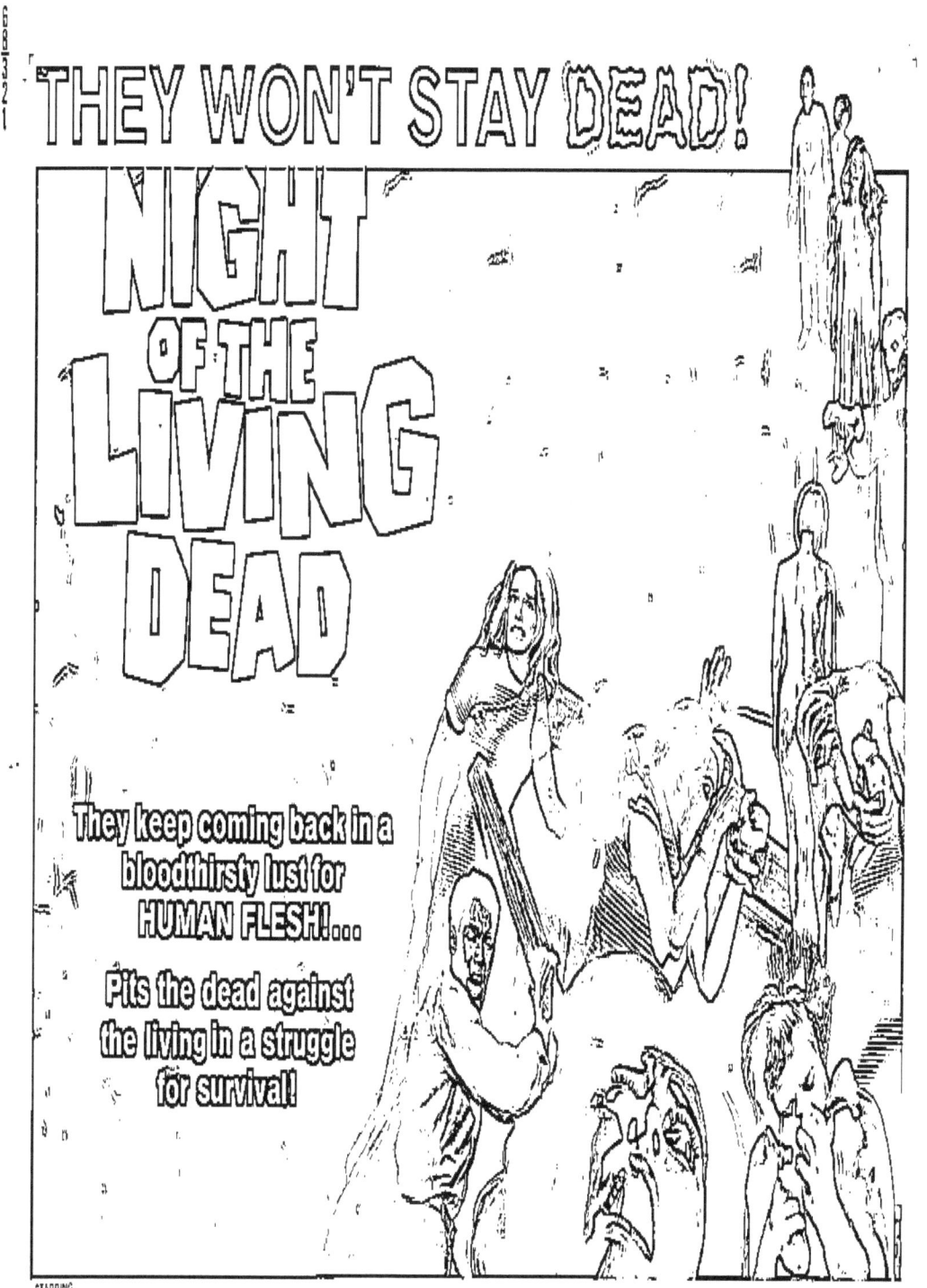

NIGHT OF THE BLOODY APES

Half Man, Half Beast, ALL HORROR!

ARMAND SILVA • NORMA LAZAR • JOE ELIAS

in a WILLIAM CALDERON production written

and directed by RENE CARDONA

a Cardona Video release

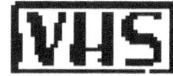

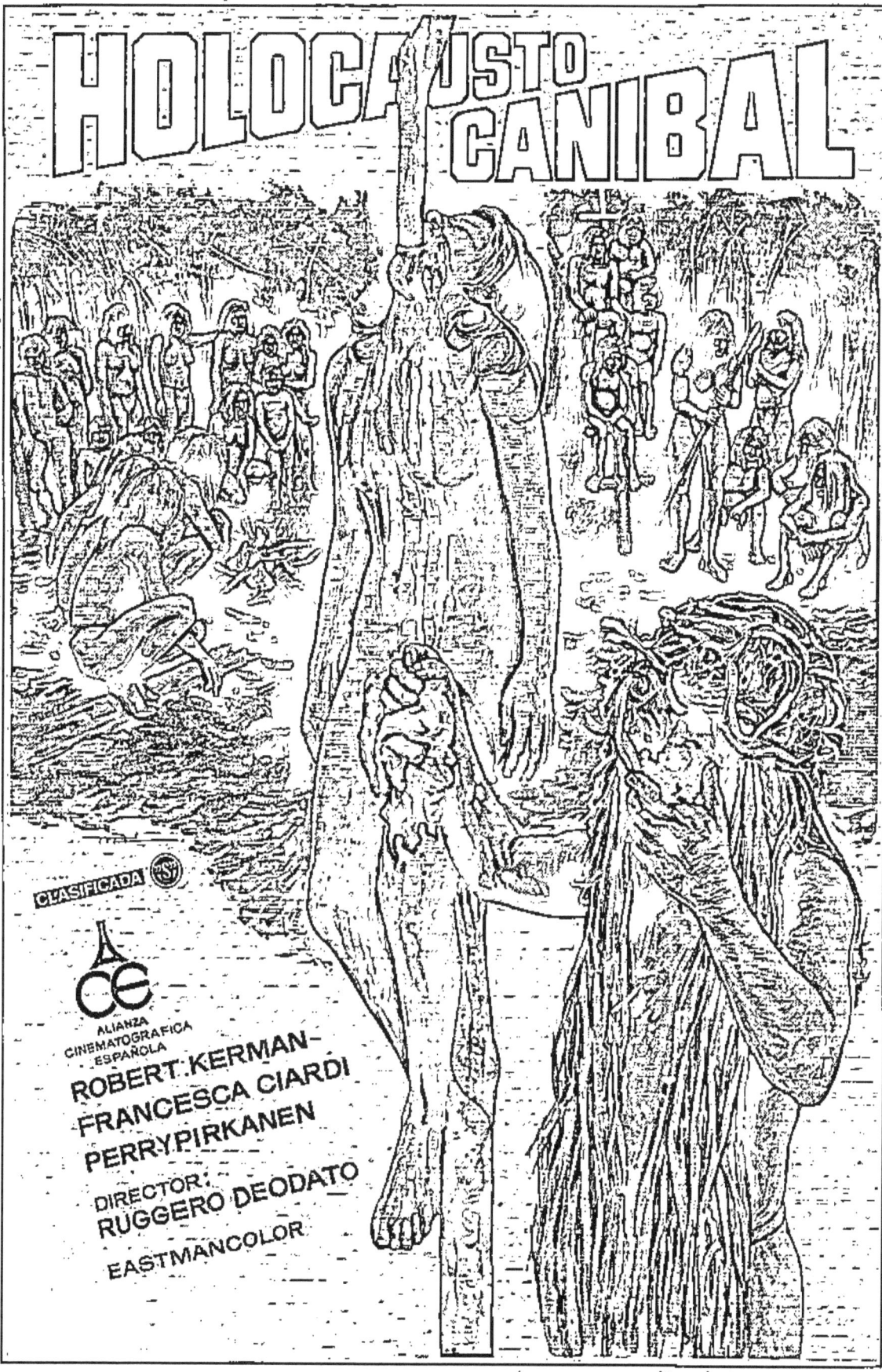

...E TU VIVRAI NEL TERRORE !

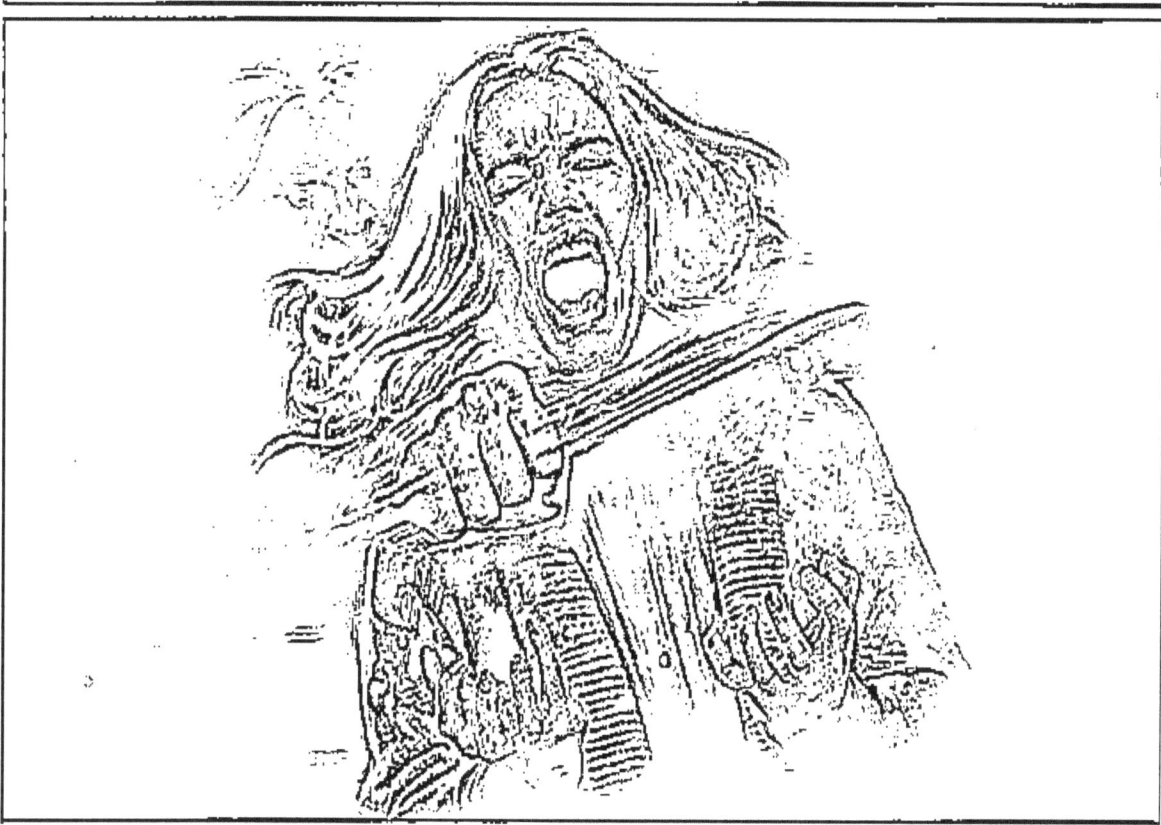

L'ALDILÀ

KATHERINE MacCOLL · DAVID WARBECK
SARAH KELLER · ANTOINE SAINT JOHN
e con **VERONICA LAZAR**

Prodotto da FABRIZIO DE ANGELIS per la FULVIA FILM srl

Regia di **LUCIO FULCI**

Technicolor

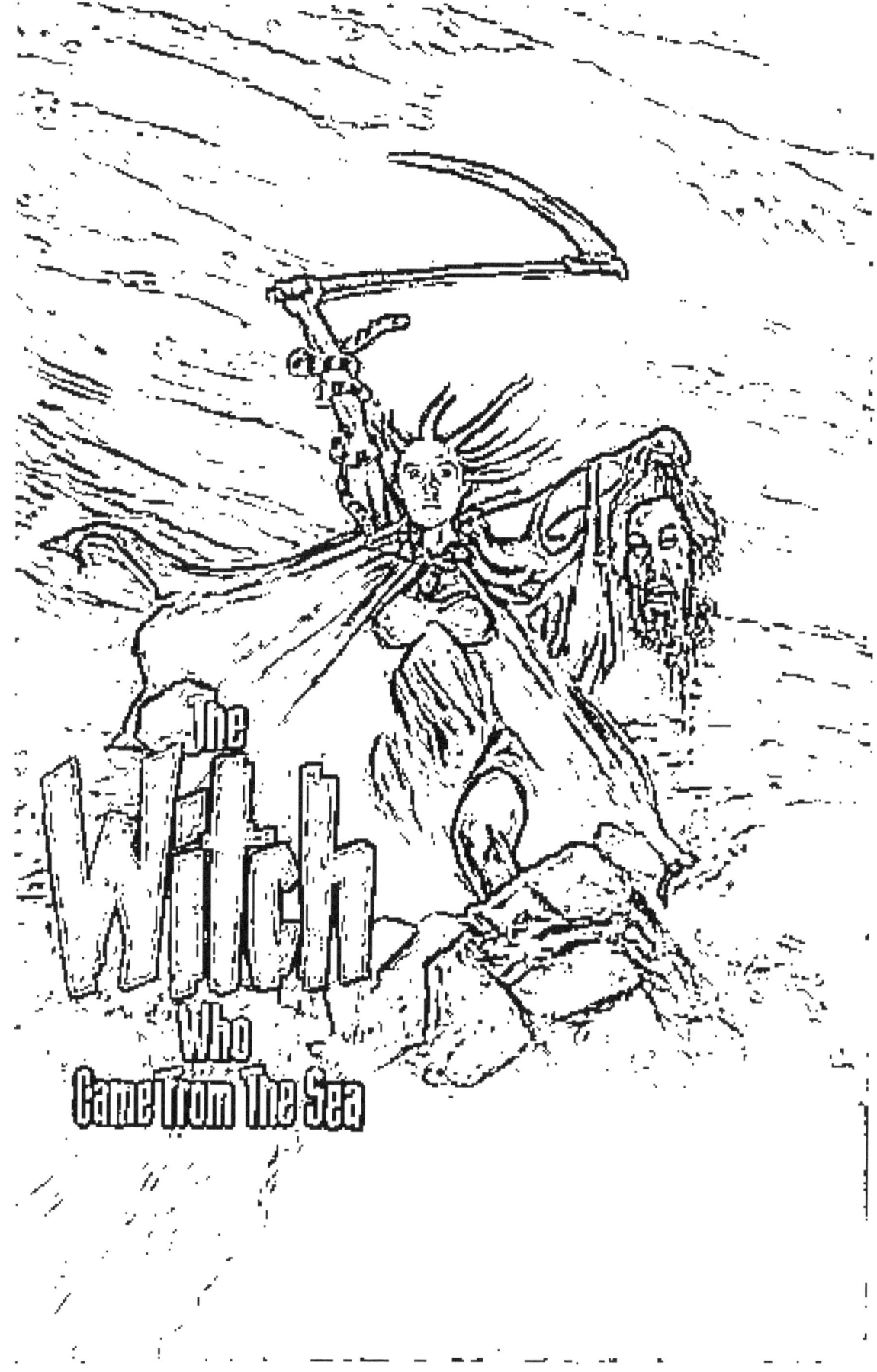

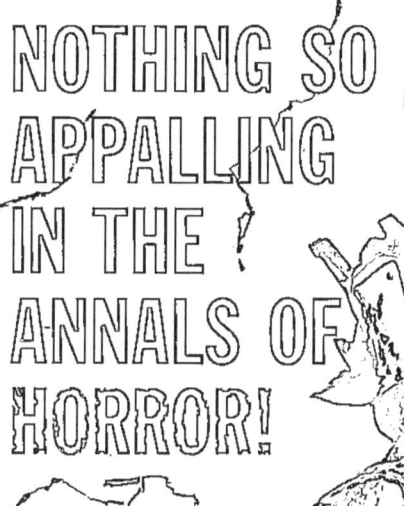
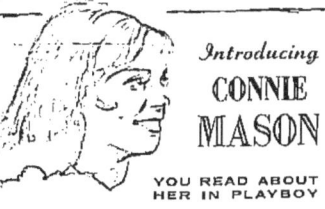

directed by
JOE D'AMATO

ANTHROPOPHAGOUS

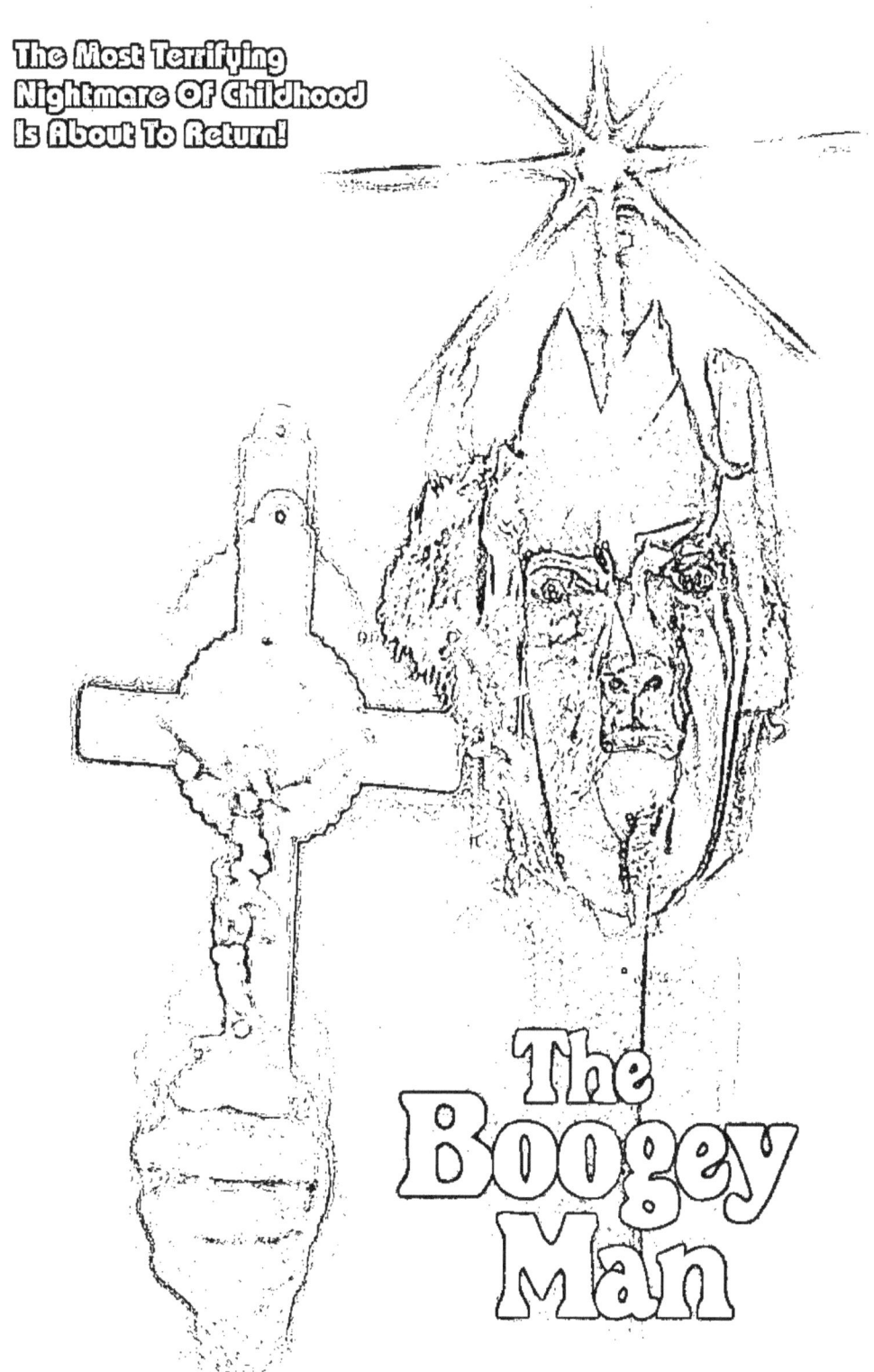

The Most Terrifying
Nightmare Of Childhood
Is About To Return!

The Boogey Man

SILVER FEROX Presents "THE BOGEYMAN"
Starring SUZANNA LOVE • RON JAMES and JOHN CARRADINE Written, Produced and Directed by ULLI LOMMEL
AN INTERBEST AMERICAN FILMS, INC. PRODUCTION COLOR by METROCOLOR

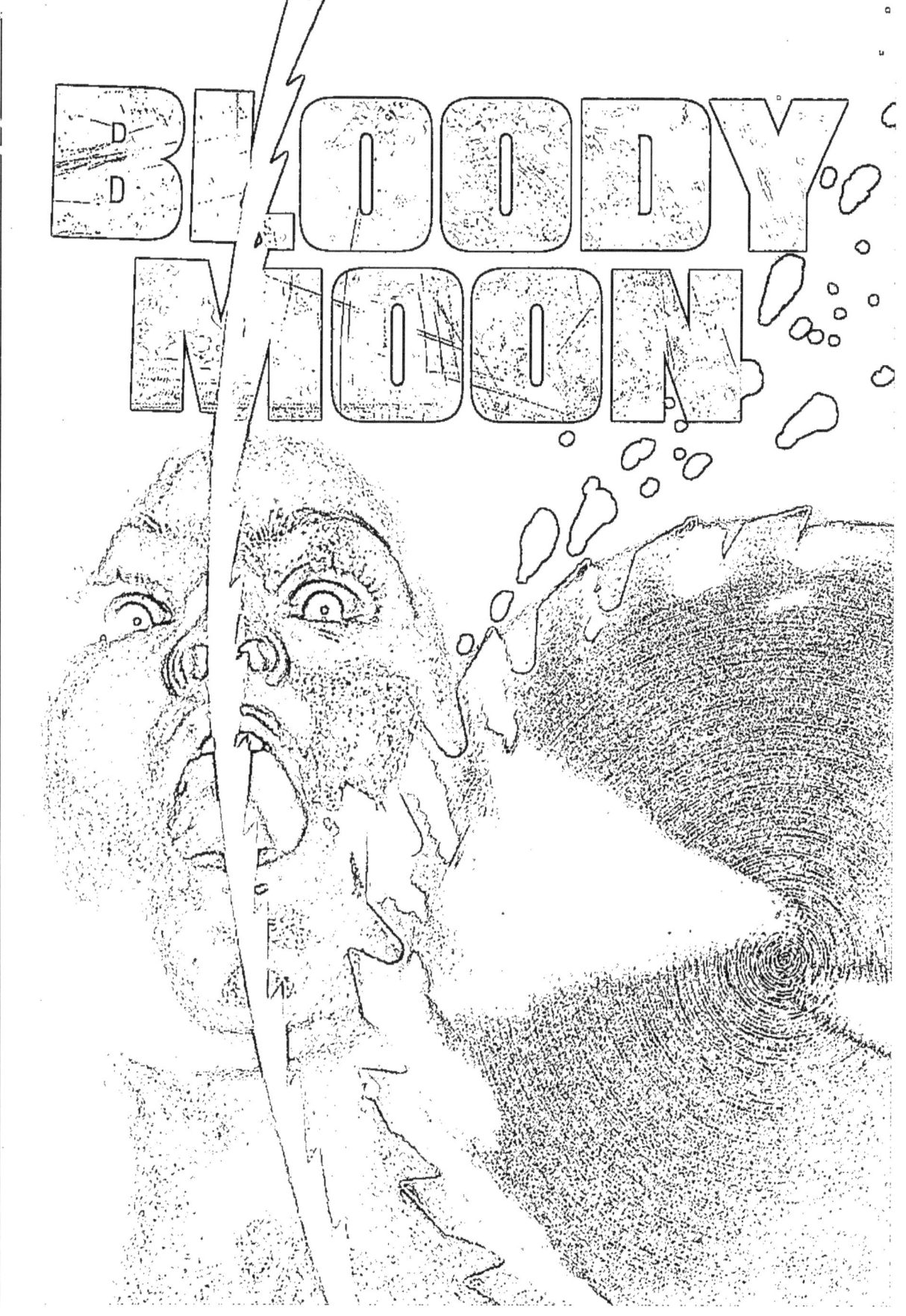

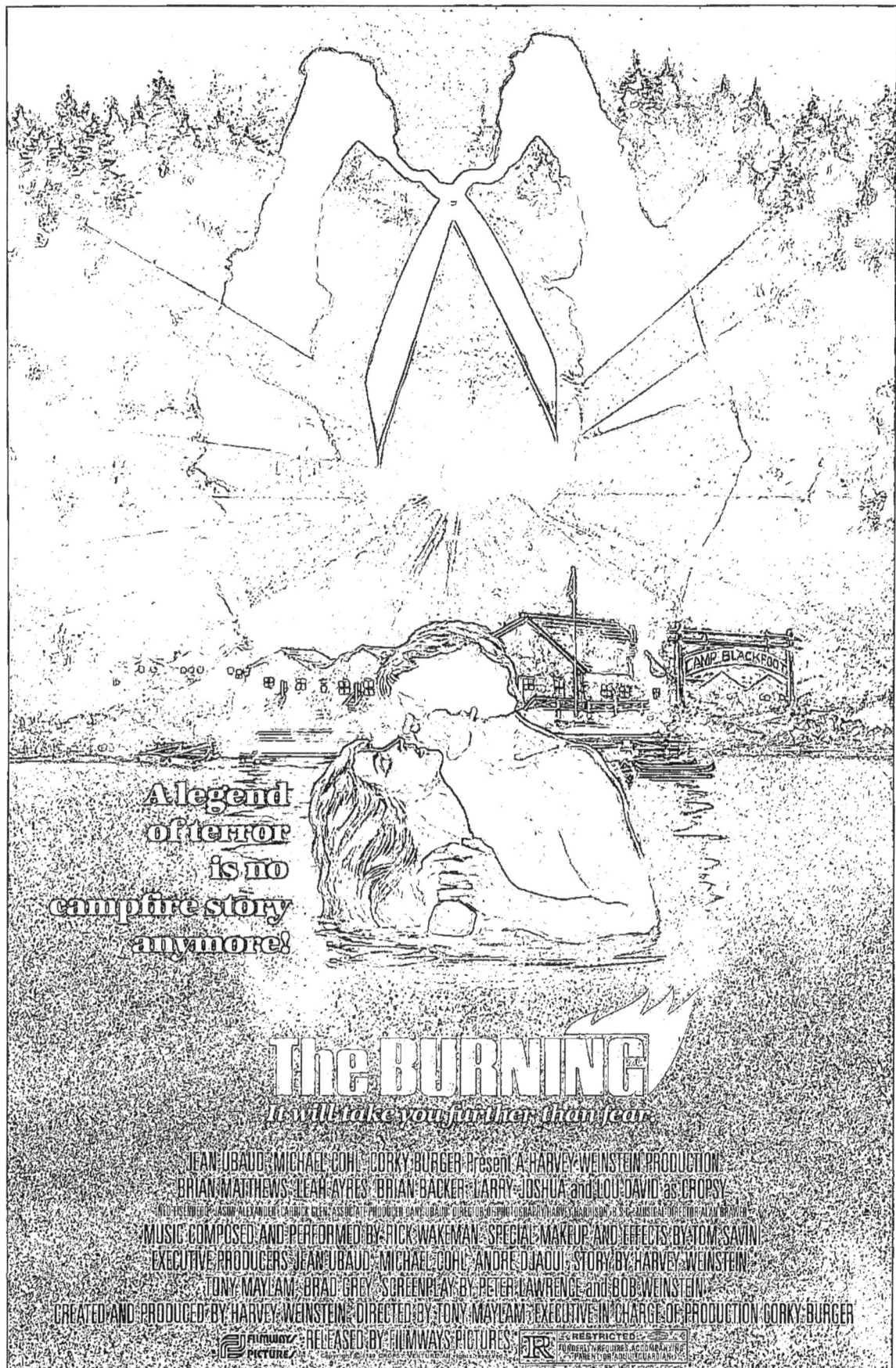

WE ARE GOING TO EAT YOU!

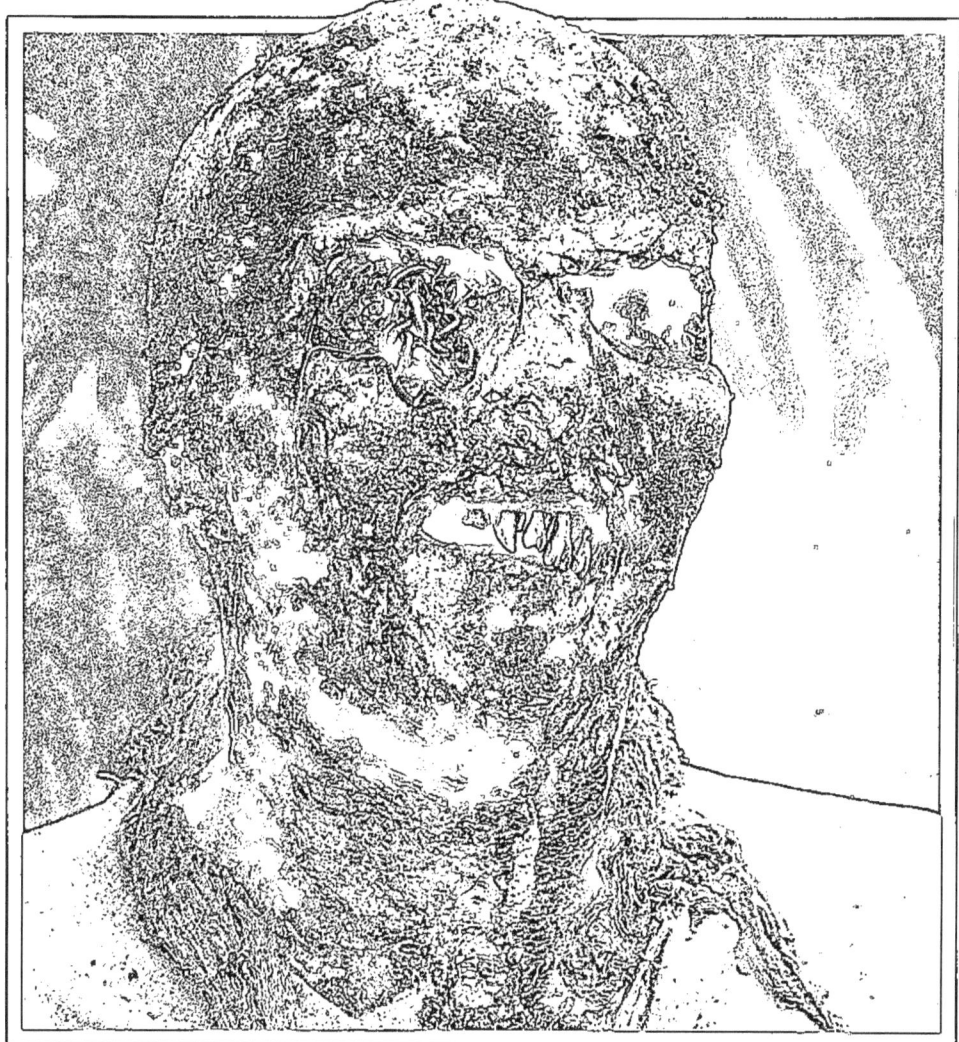

ZOMBIE

...THE DEAD ARE AMONG US!

Jerry Gross presents "ZOMBIE" starring Tisa Farrow ○ Ian McCulloch ○ Richard Johnson ○ Al Cliver
Story and Screenplay by Elisa Briganti ○ Produced by Ugo Tucci and Fabrizio De Angelis for Variety Film
Color by Metro Color ○ Directed by Lucio Fulci ○ Distributed by The Jerry Gross Organization

There is no explicit sex in this picture.
However, there are scenes of violence which may be considered shocking.
No one under 17 will be admitted.

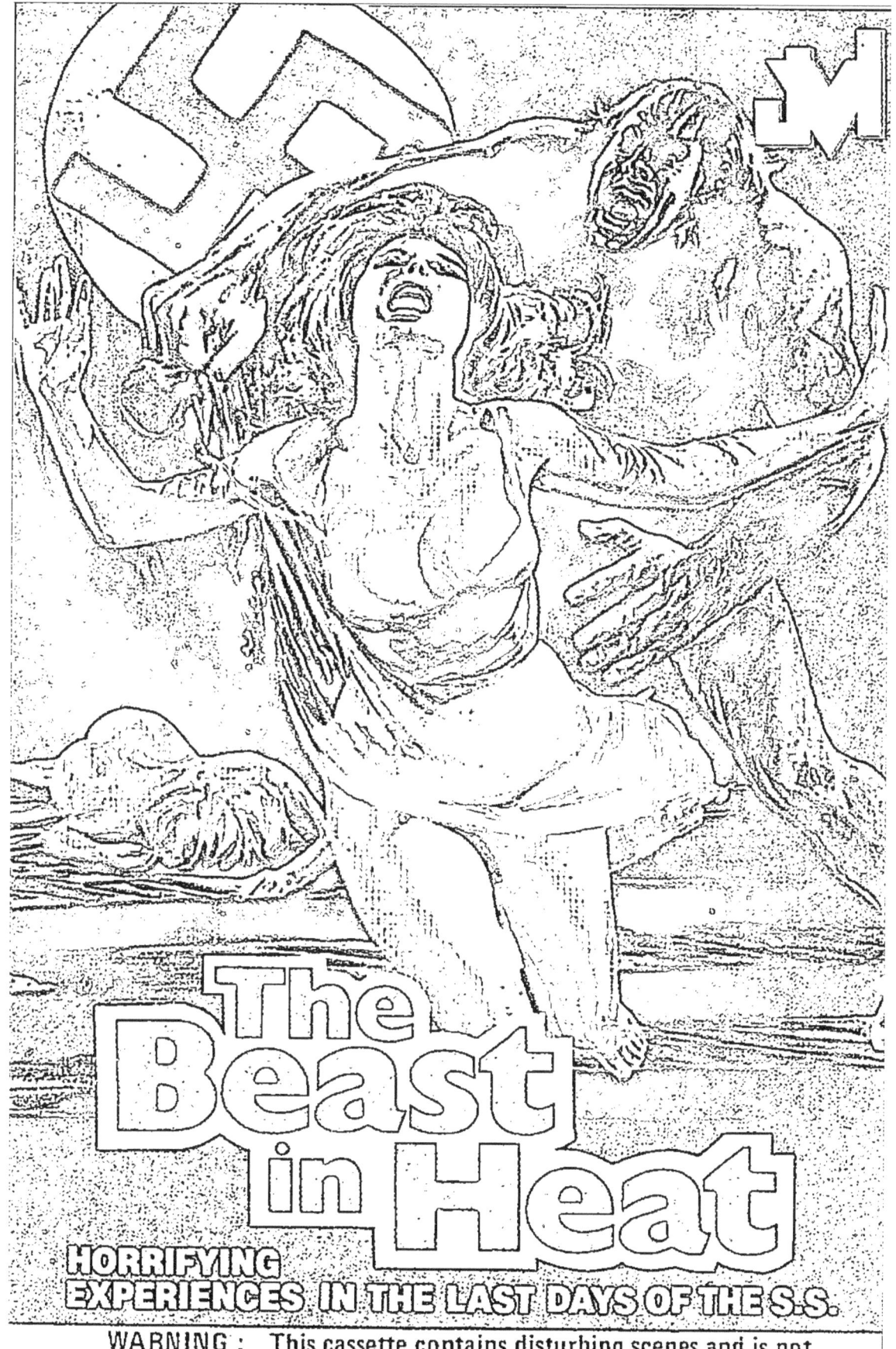

The Beast in Heat

HORRIFYING EXPERIENCES IN THE LAST DAYS OF THE S.S.

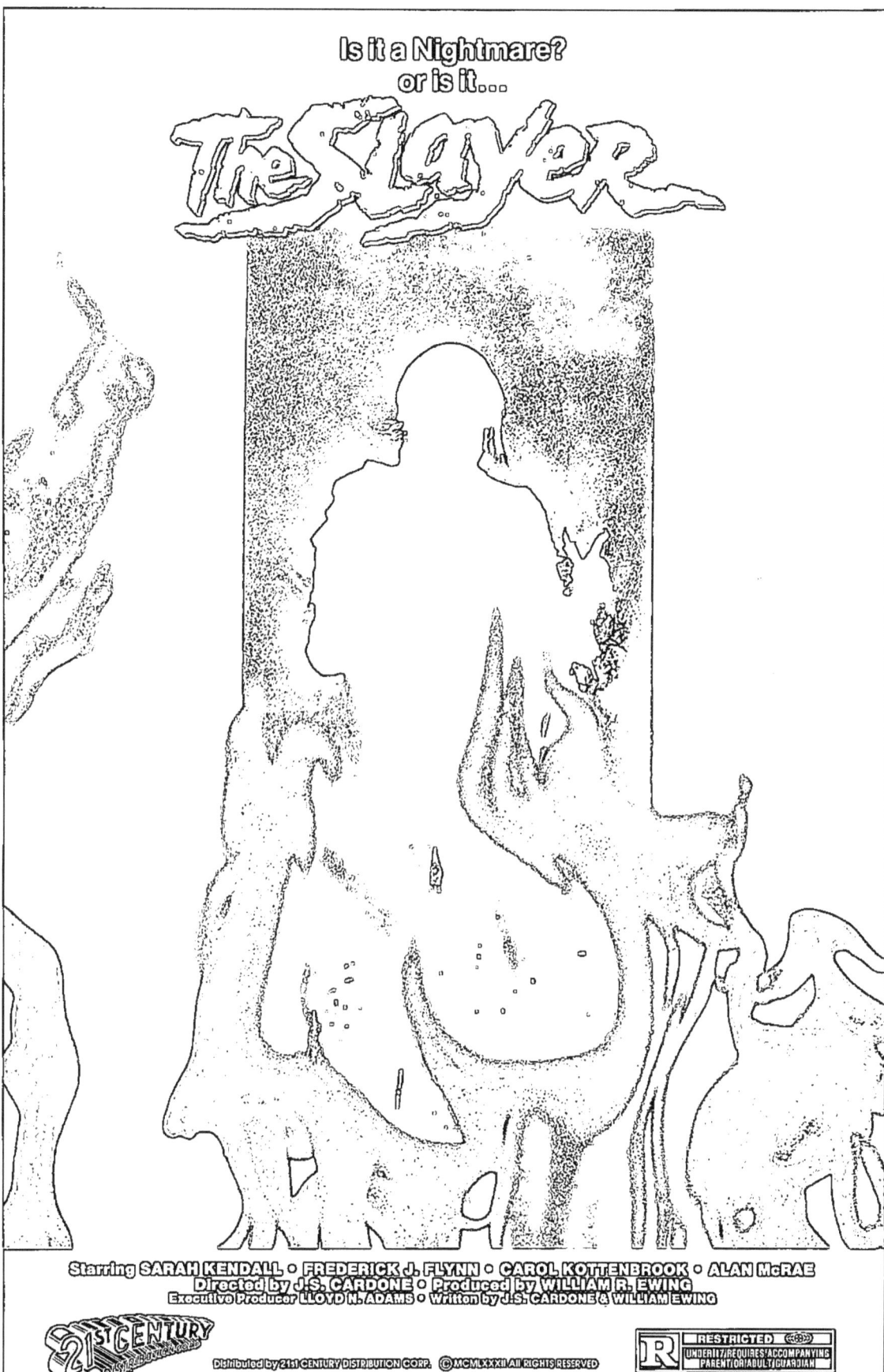

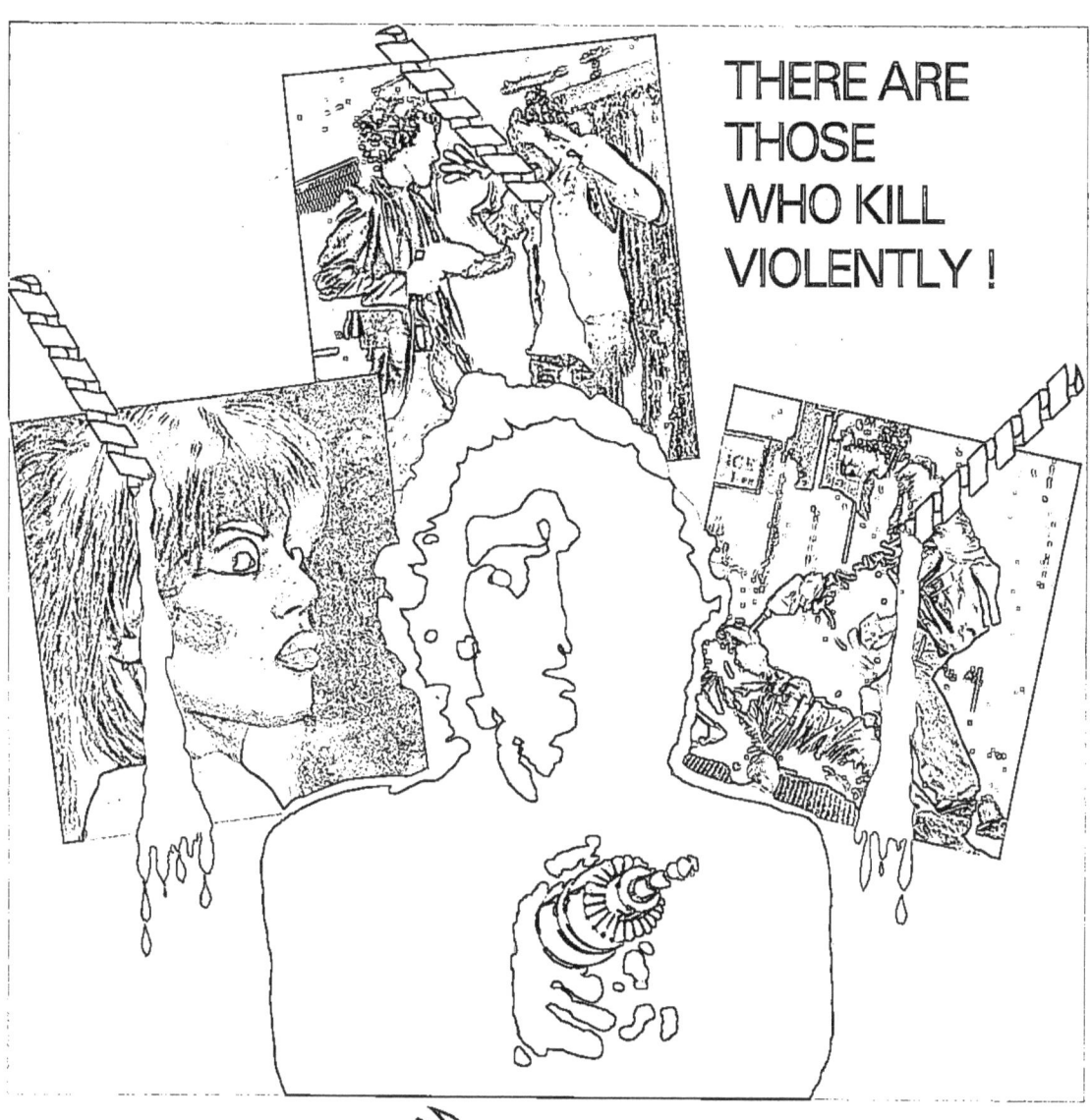

THERE ARE
THOSE
WHO KILL
VIOLENTLY !

DRLLER
KLLER

This motion picture has been deemed TOO VIOLENT to
be accorded a motion picture rating. There are no explicit
sexual scenes. However, due to the violent nature of this
film NO ONE UNDER 17 WILL BE ADMITTED WITHOUT
BEING ACCOMPANIED BY A PARENT OR GUARDIAN.

ROCHELLE FILMS presents A NAVARON FILM PRODUCTION
Starring CAROLYN MARZ • JIMMY LAINE • BAYBI DAY
with BOB DE FRANK • PETER YELLEN • HARRY SCHULTZ
and featuring TONY COCA COLA AND THE ROOSTERS • Screenplay by NICHOLAS ST. JOHN
Music by JOSEPH DELIA • Director of Photography KEN KELSCH Sound J.P. MAC INTYRE
Executive Producer ROCHELLE WEISBERG • Produced by NAVARON FILMS • Directed by ABEL FERRARA

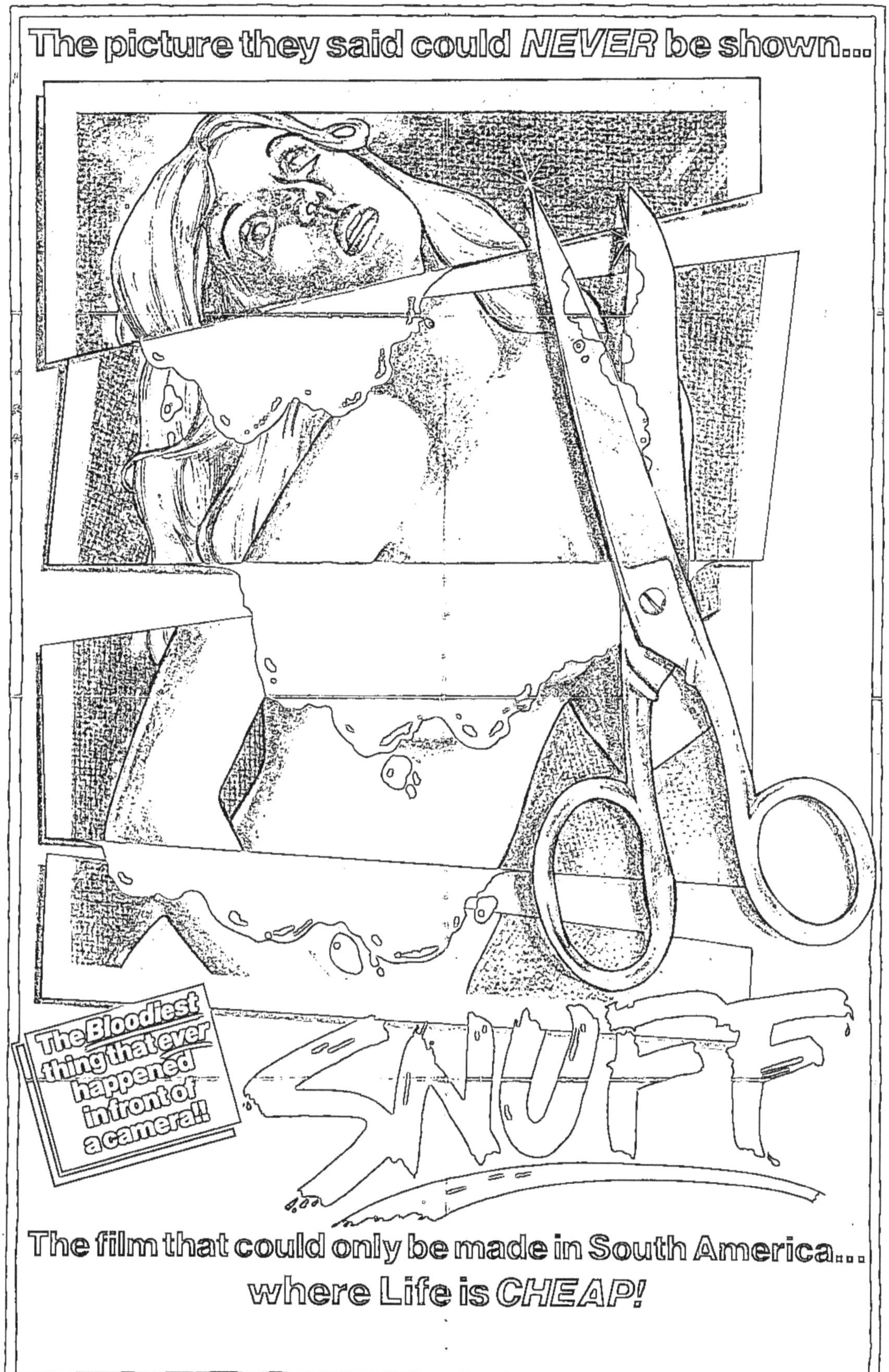
The picture they said could NEVER be shown...
The Bloodiest thing that ever happened infront of a camera!!
SNUFF
The film that could only be made in South America...
where Life is CHEAP!

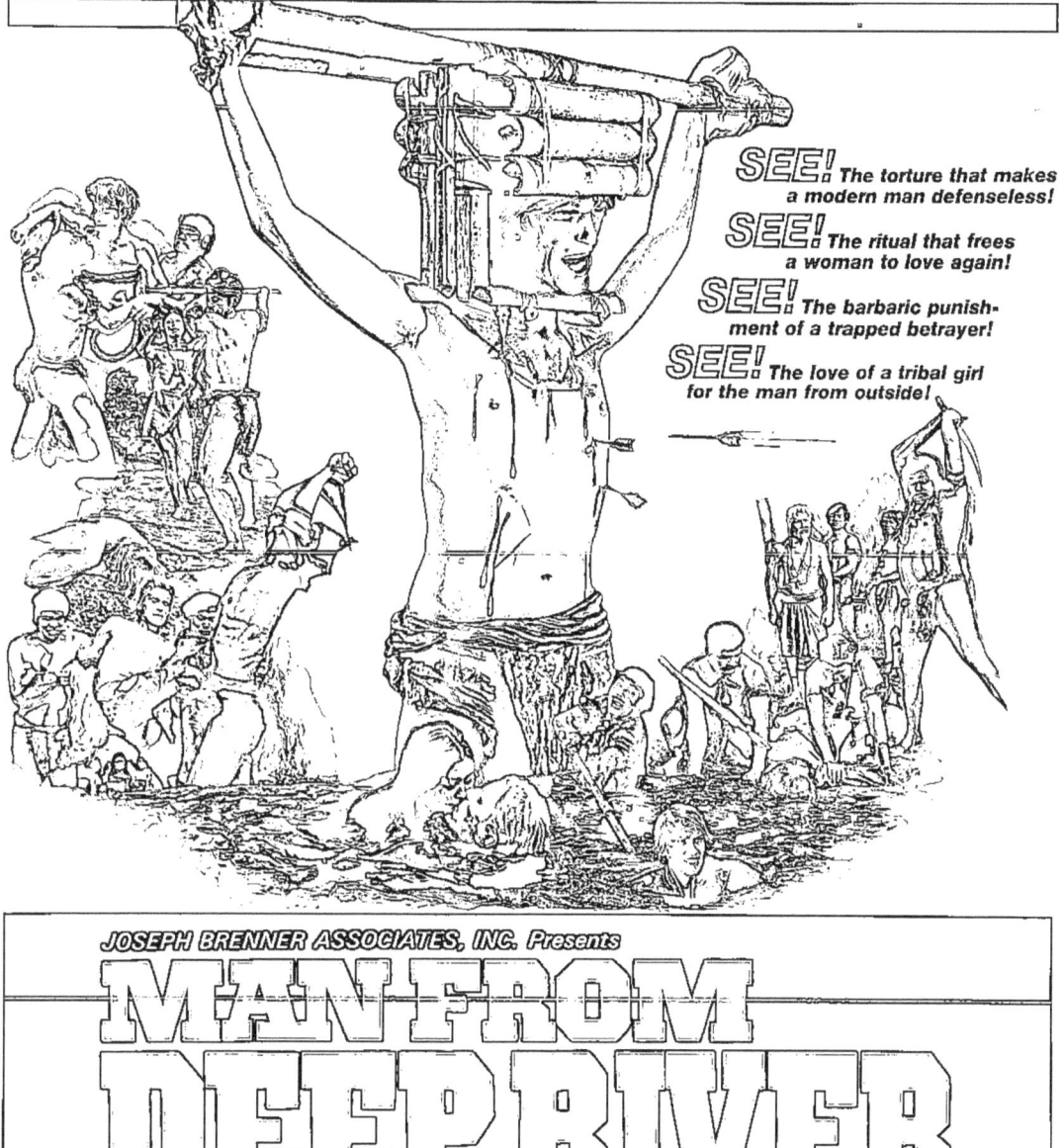

He dared the forbidden river!
WHERE ADVENTURE ENDS ...AND HELL BEGINS!

SEE! The torture that makes a modern man defenseless!

SEE! The ritual that frees a woman to love again!

SEE! The barbaric punishment of a trapped betrayer!

SEE! The love of a tribal girl for the man from outside!

JOSEPH BRENNER ASSOCIATES, INC. Presents

MAN FROM DEEP RIVER

MAN FROM DEEP RIVER Starring IVAN RASSIMOV/ME ME LAY

Directed by   Produced by
UMBERTO LENZI/ GIORGIO C. ROSSI/OVIDIO G. ASSONITIS FOR ROAS PRODUCTIONS/MEDUSA
A JOSEPH BRENNER ASSOCIATES, INC. RELEASE **TECHNICOLOR®/TECHNISCOPE®**

MAN FROM DEEP RIVER

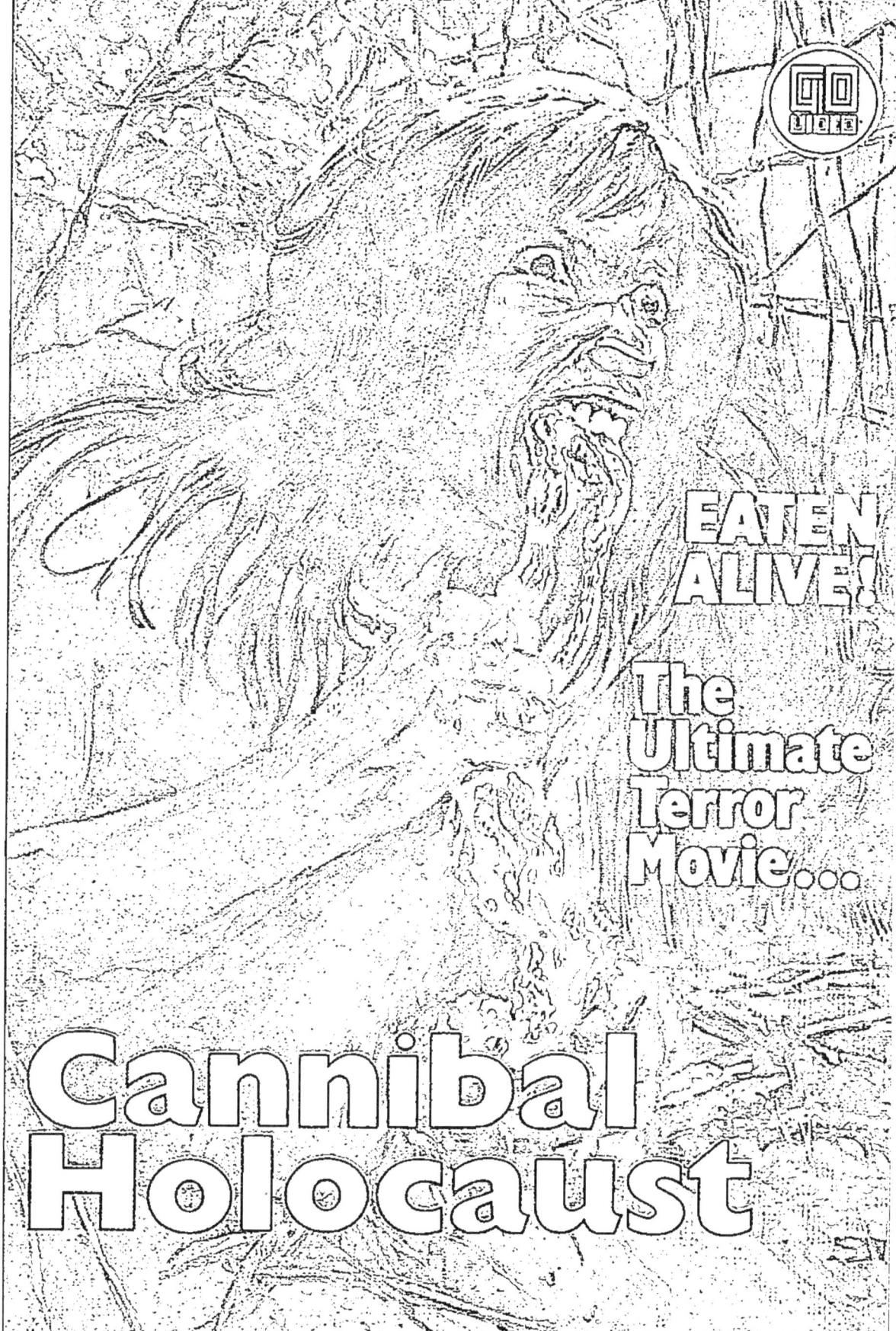

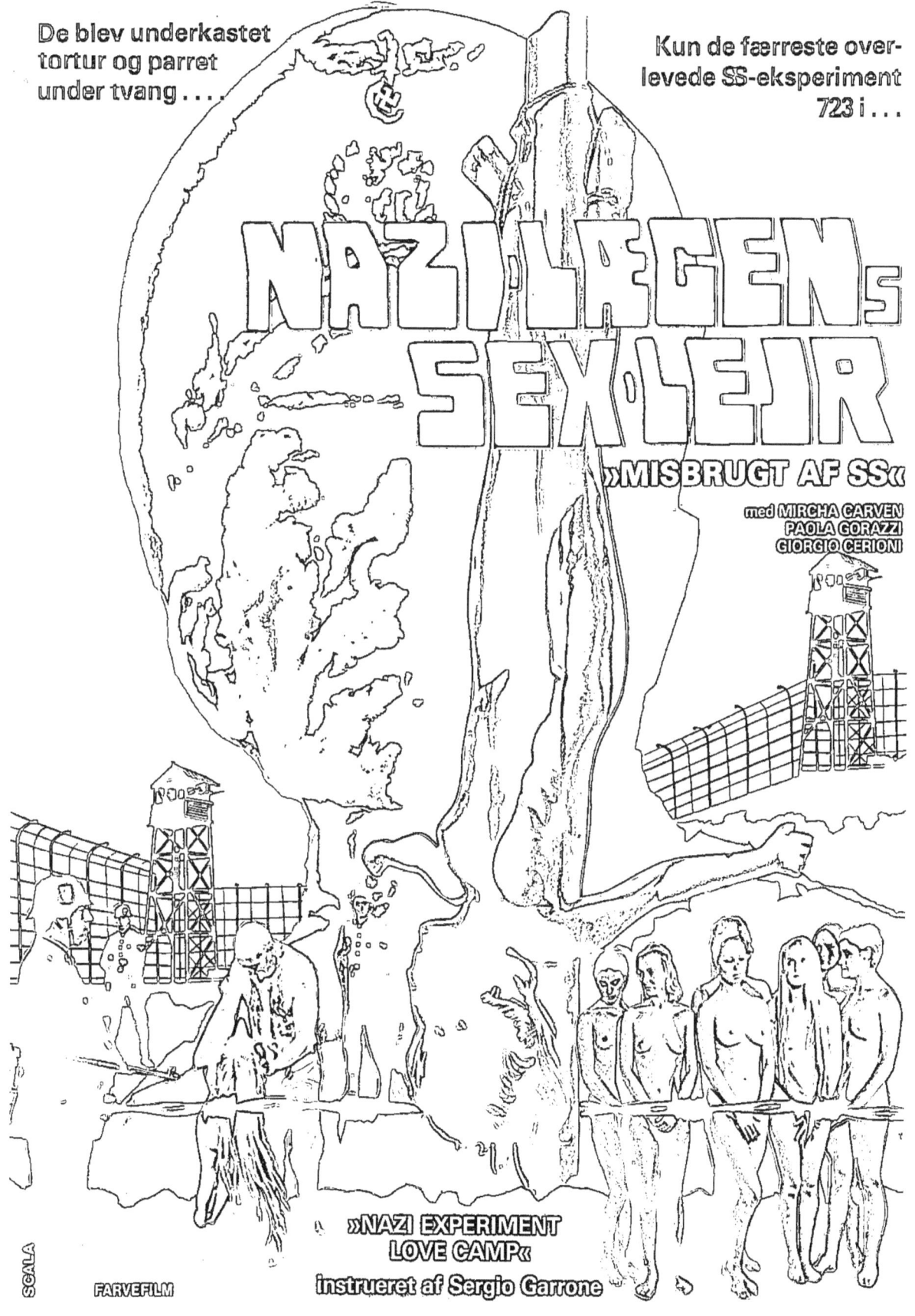

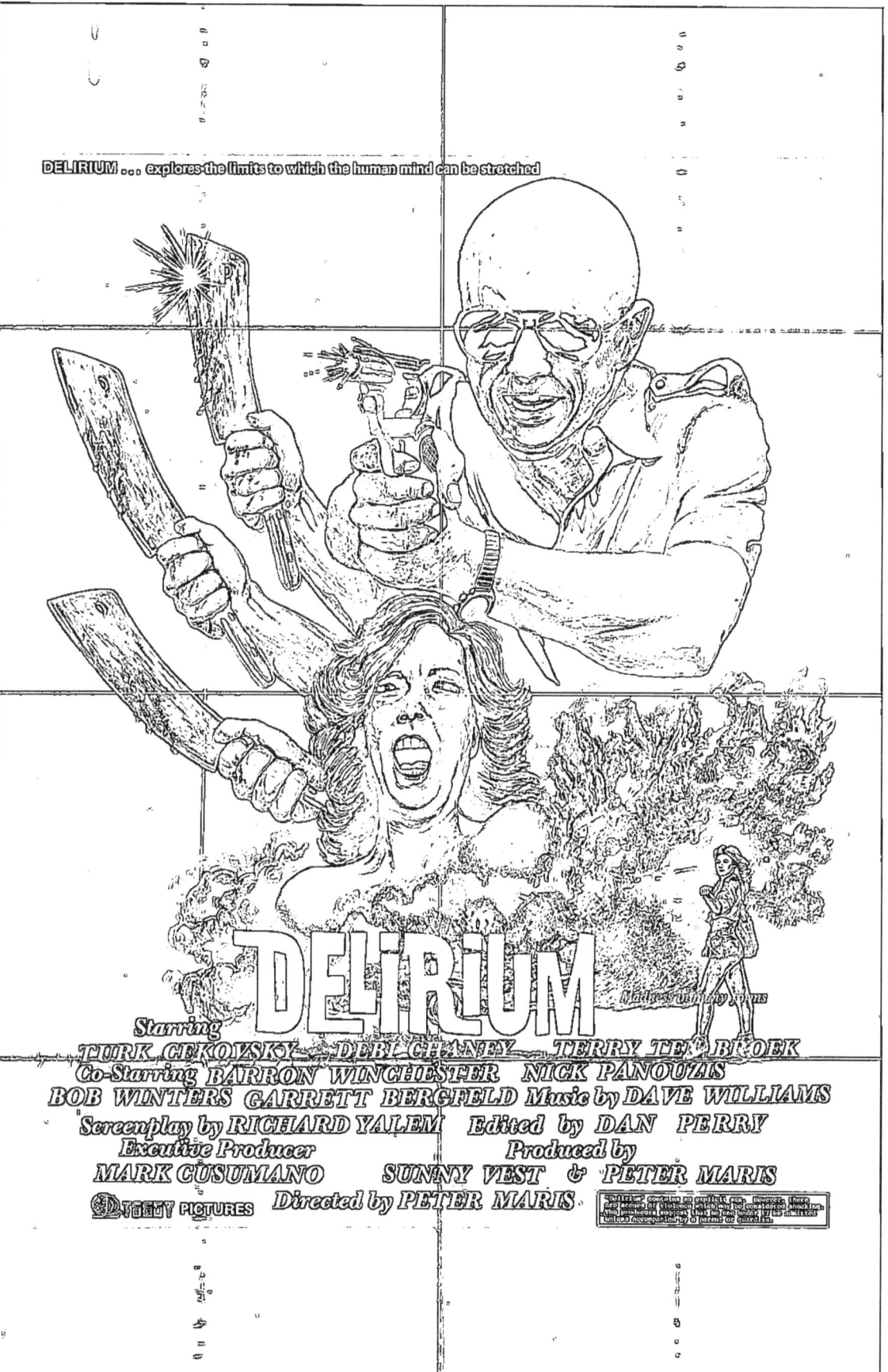

BIZARRE HUMAN SACRIFICES!
The most Violent Film Ever!

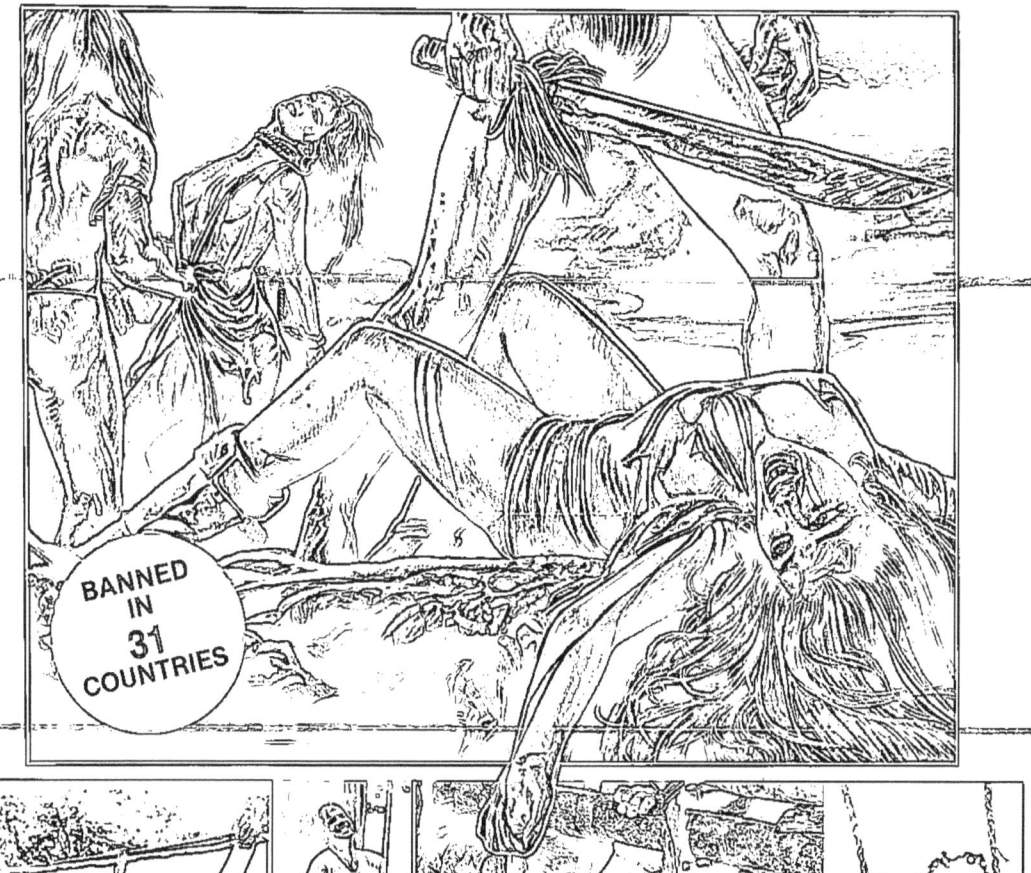

BANNED IN 31 COUNTRIES

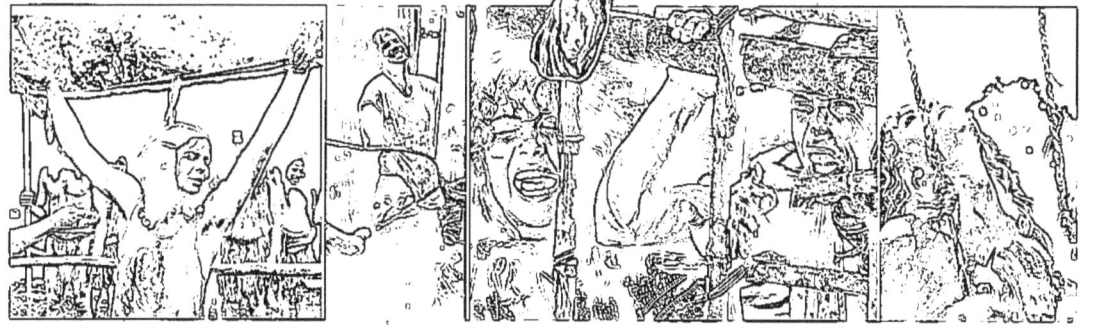

THEY RAPED & MURDERED HIS SISTER WHILE HE WATCHED HELPLESSLY.
NOW IT'S HIS TURN TO...

MAKE THEM DIE SLOWLY

Starring
JOHN MORGHEN • LORAINNE DE SELLE • BRIAN REDFORD
ZORA KEROWA • ROBERT KERMAN • JOHN BARTHA
WALTER LLOYD • MEG FLEMMING • VENANTINO VANANTINI

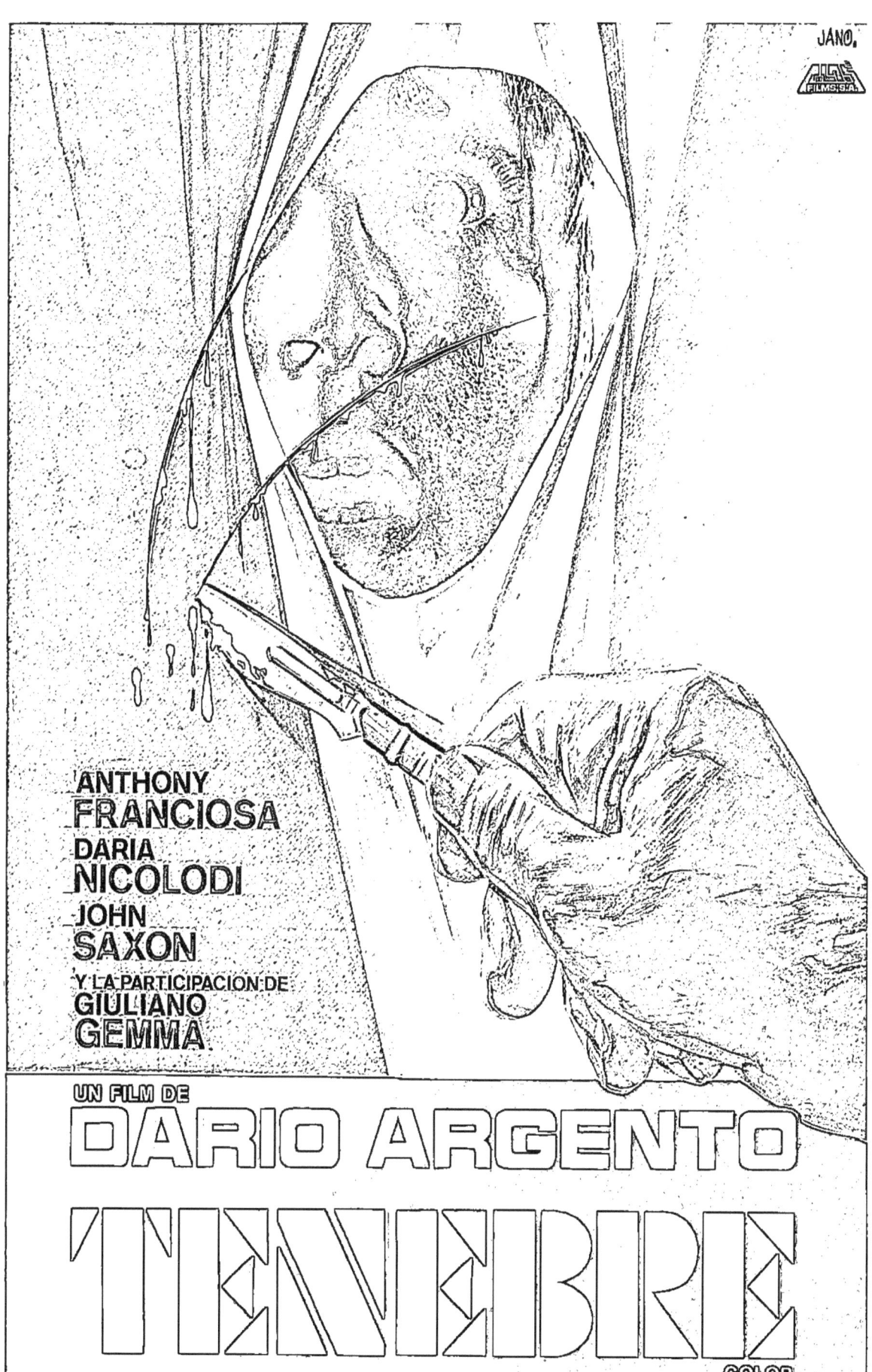

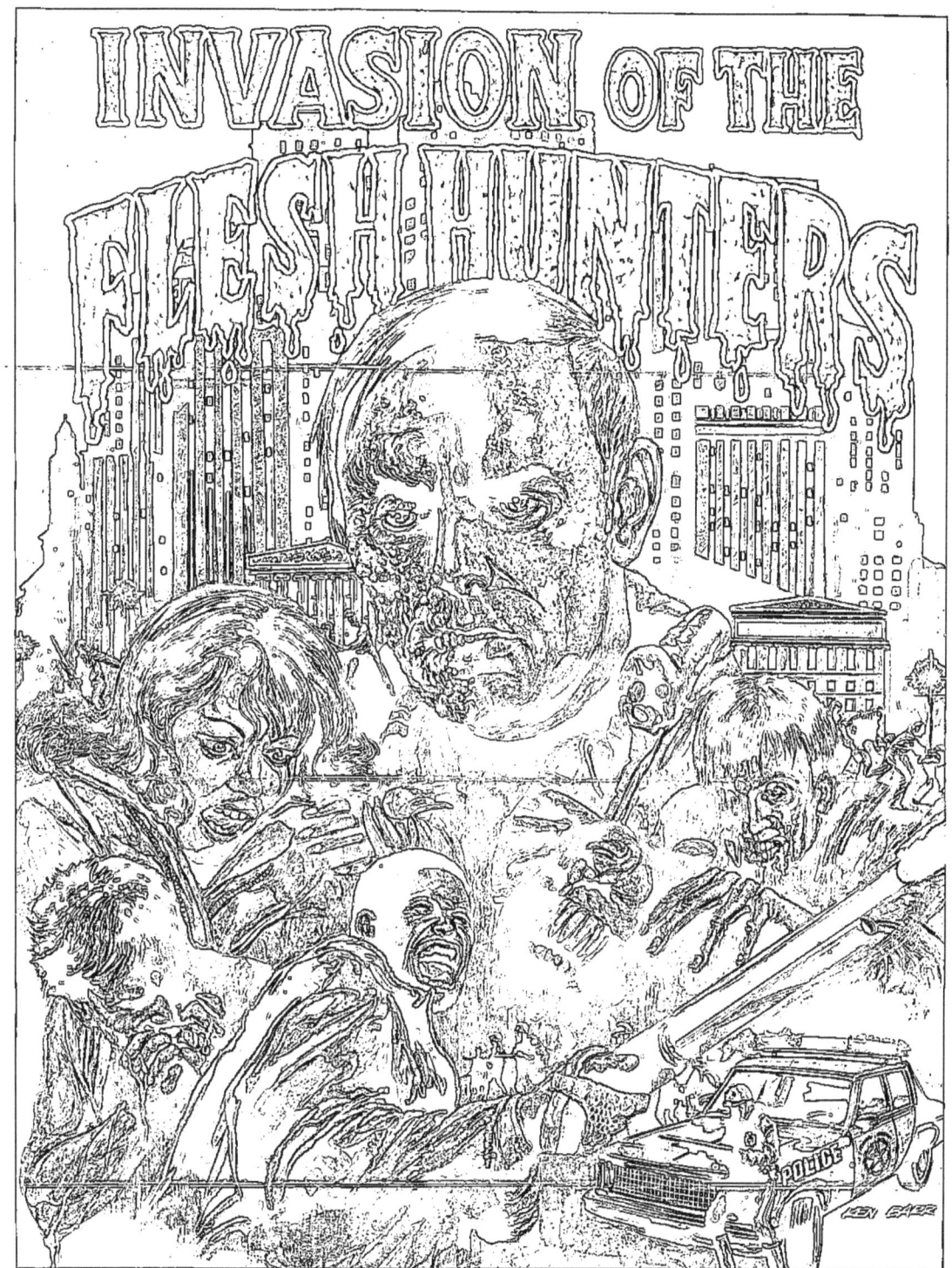

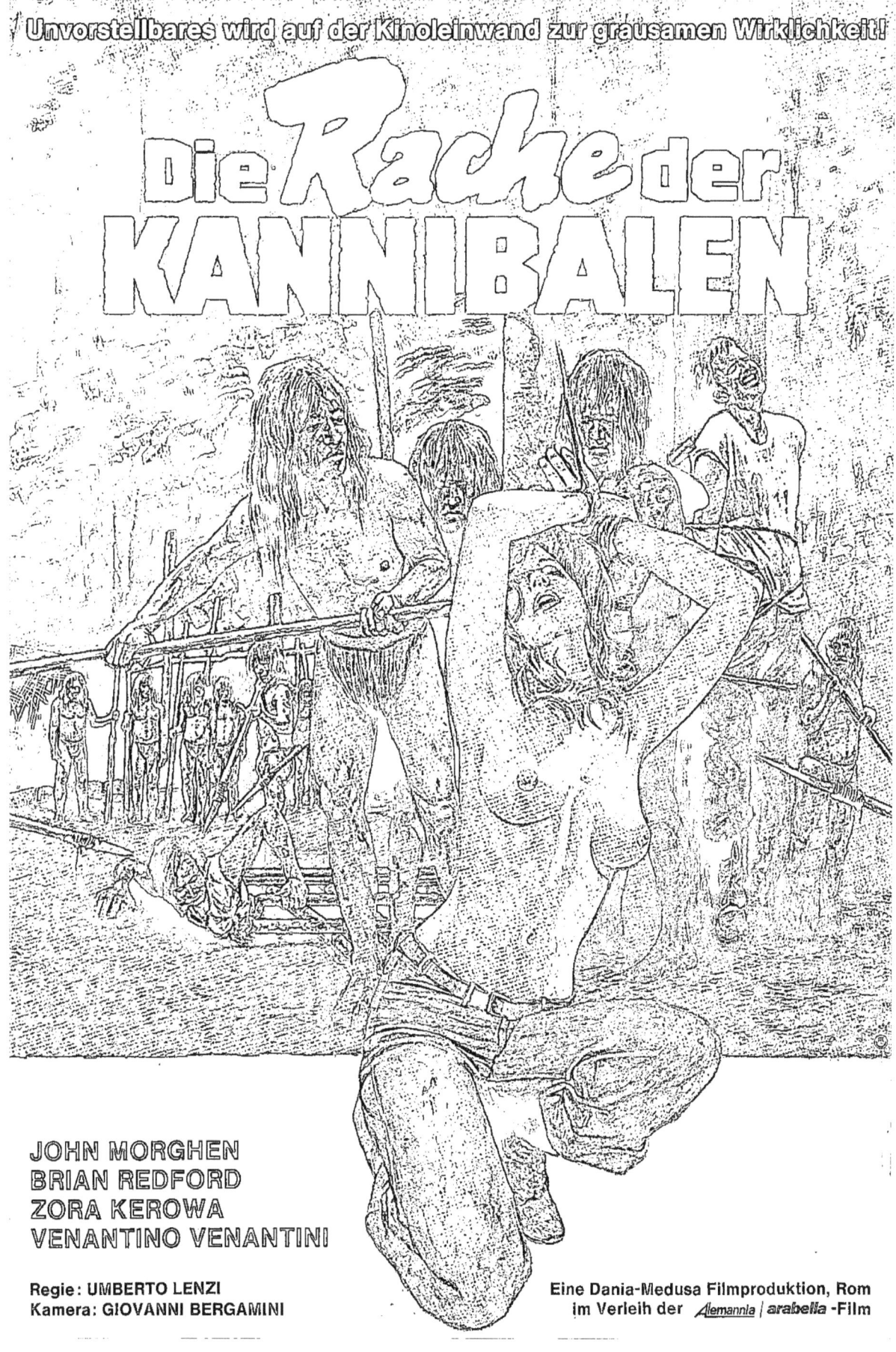

Unvorstellbares wird auf der Kinoleinwand zur grausamen Wirklichkeit!

Die Rache der KANNIBALEN

JOHN MORGHEN
BRIAN REDFORD
ZORA KEROWA
VENANTINO VENANTINI

Regie: UMBERTO LENZI
Kamera: GIOVANNI BERGAMINI

Eine Dania-Medusa Filmproduktion, Rom
im Verleih der Alemannia | arabella -Film

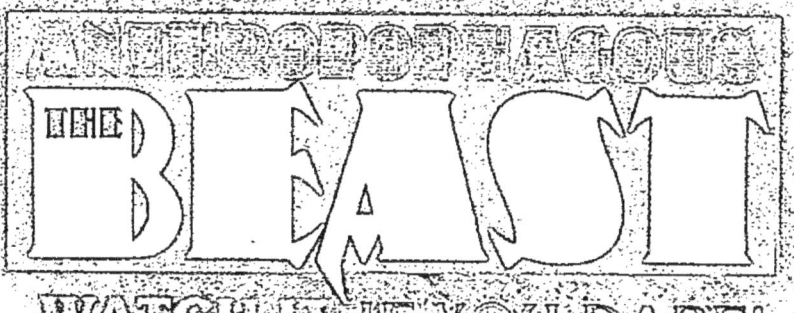

ANTHROPOPHAGOUS

THE BEAST

WATCH IT IF YOU DARE!

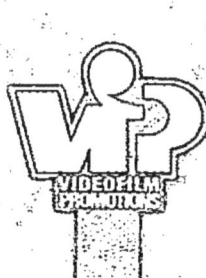

A film by JOE D'AMATO
starring GEORGE EASTMAN and
TISA FARROW
Running time 1 hr. and 30 mins. approx. Colour.

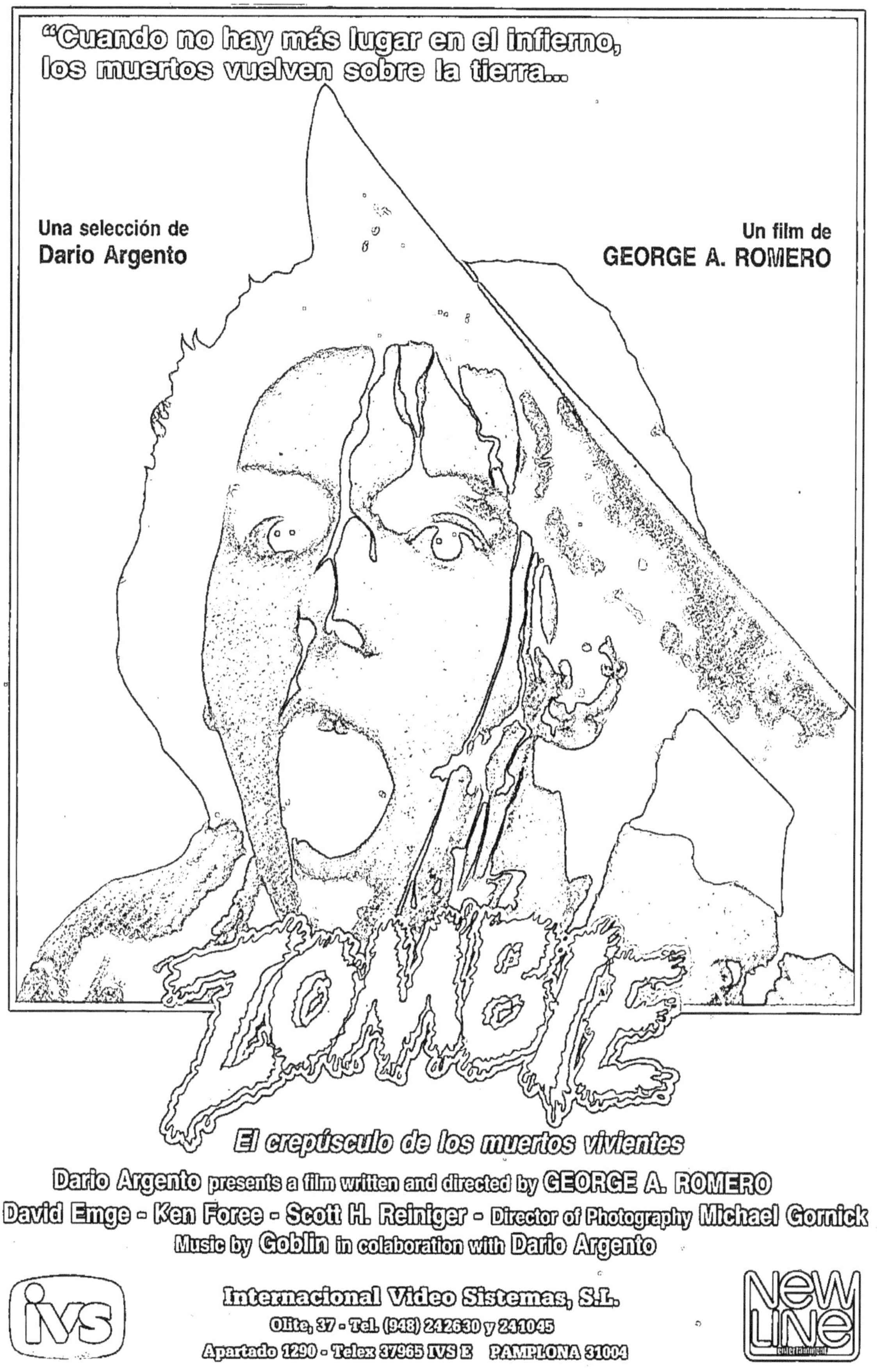

"Cuando no hay más lugar en el infierno,
los muertos vuelven sobre la tierra...

Una selección de
Dario Argento

Un film de
GEORGE A. ROMERO

El crepúsculo de los muertos vivientes

Dario Argento presents a film written and directed by GEORGE A. ROMERO

David Emge - Ken Foree - Scott H. Reiniger - Director of Photography Michael Gornick

Music by Goblin in colaboration with Dario Argento

Internacional Video Sistemas, S.L.
Olite, 37 - Tel. (948) 242630 y 241045
Apartado 1290 - Telex 37965 IVS E   PAMPLONA 31004

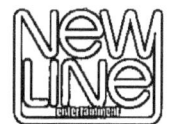

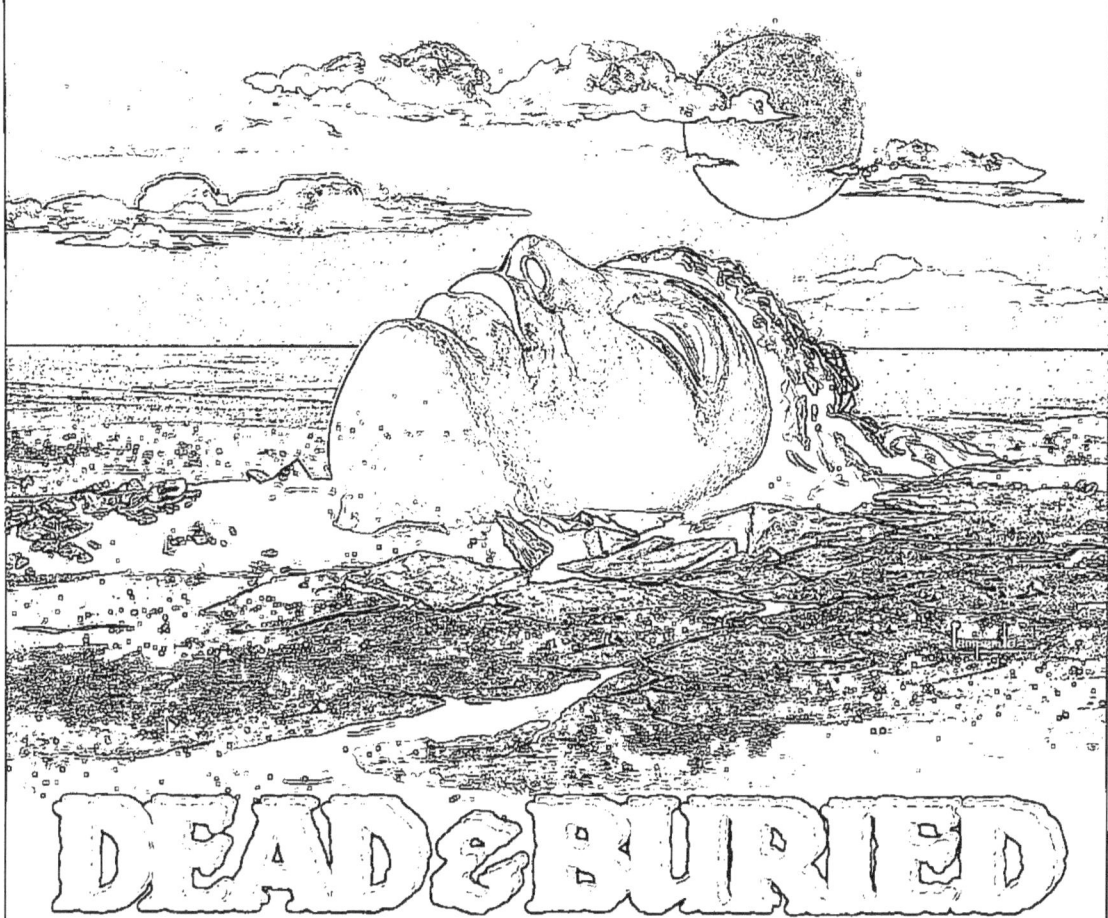

The creators of ALIEN...
...bring a new terror to Earth.

DEAD & BURIED

It will take your breath away...all of it.

RICHARD R. ST. JOHNS PRESENTS
A RONALD SHUSETT PRODUCTION
DEAD & BURIED
STARRING JAMES FARENTINO MELODY ANDERSON AND JACK ALBERTSON
SCREENPLAY BY RONALD SHUSETT AND DAN O'BANNON BASED UPON A STORY BY JEFF MILLAR AND ALEX STERN
PRODUCED BY RONALD SHUSETT AND ROBERT FENTRESS DIRECTED BY GARY A. SHERMAN
EXECUTIVE PRODUCER RICHARD R. ST. JOHNS MUSIC BY JOE RENZETTI MAKE UP EFFECTS DESIGNED BY STAN WINSTON
EXECUTIVE IN CHARGE OF PRODUCTION JOHN W. HYDE AVCO EMBASSY PICTURES Release AVAILABLE IN PAPERBACK FROM WARNER BOOKS LENSES AND PANAFLEX CAMERA BY PANAVISION® [R] RESTRICTED UNDER 17 REQUIRES ACCOMPANYING PARENT OR ADULT GUARDIAN
Prints by CFI COLOR BY TECHNICOLOR® ©1981 BARCLAYS MERCANTILE INDUSTRIAL FINANCE LIMITED ©1981 AVCO EMBASSY PICTURES CORP.

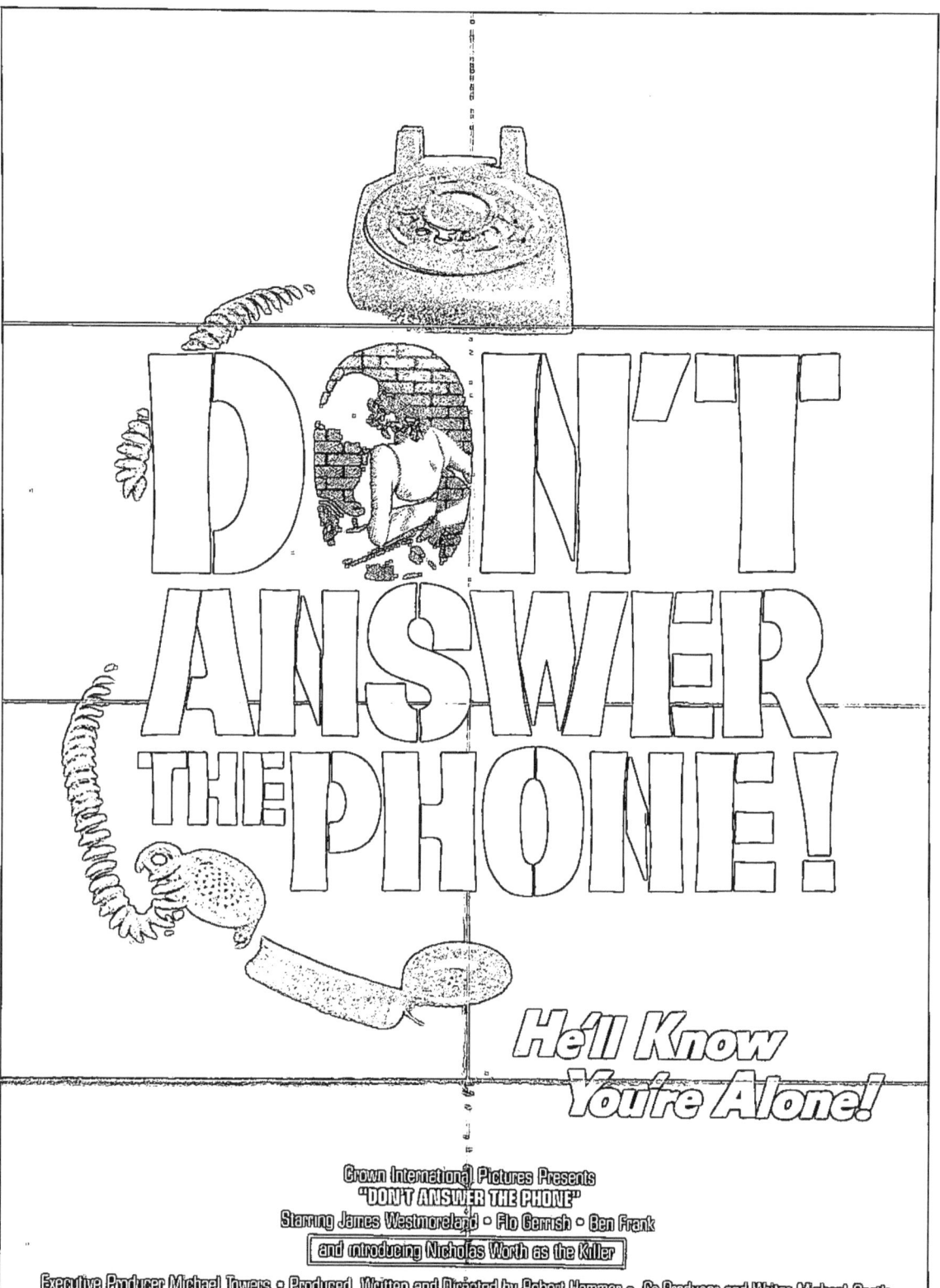

DON'T ANSWER THE PHONE!

He'll Know
You're Alone!

Crown International Pictures Presents
"DON'T ANSWER THE PHONE"
Starring James Westmoreland • Flo Gerrish • Ben Frank
and introducing Nicholas Worth as the Killer

Executive Producer Michael Towers • Produced, Written and Directed by Robert Hammer • Co-Producer and Writer Michael Castle
Director of Photography James Carter   Edited by Joseph Fineman   Music by Byron Allred

A Scorpion Production • A Crown International Pictures Release   METROCOLOR®   R RESTRICTED ⬚ UNDER 17 REQUIRES ACCOMPANYING PARENT OR ADULT GUARDIAN

800033

"DON'T ANSWER THE PHONE"

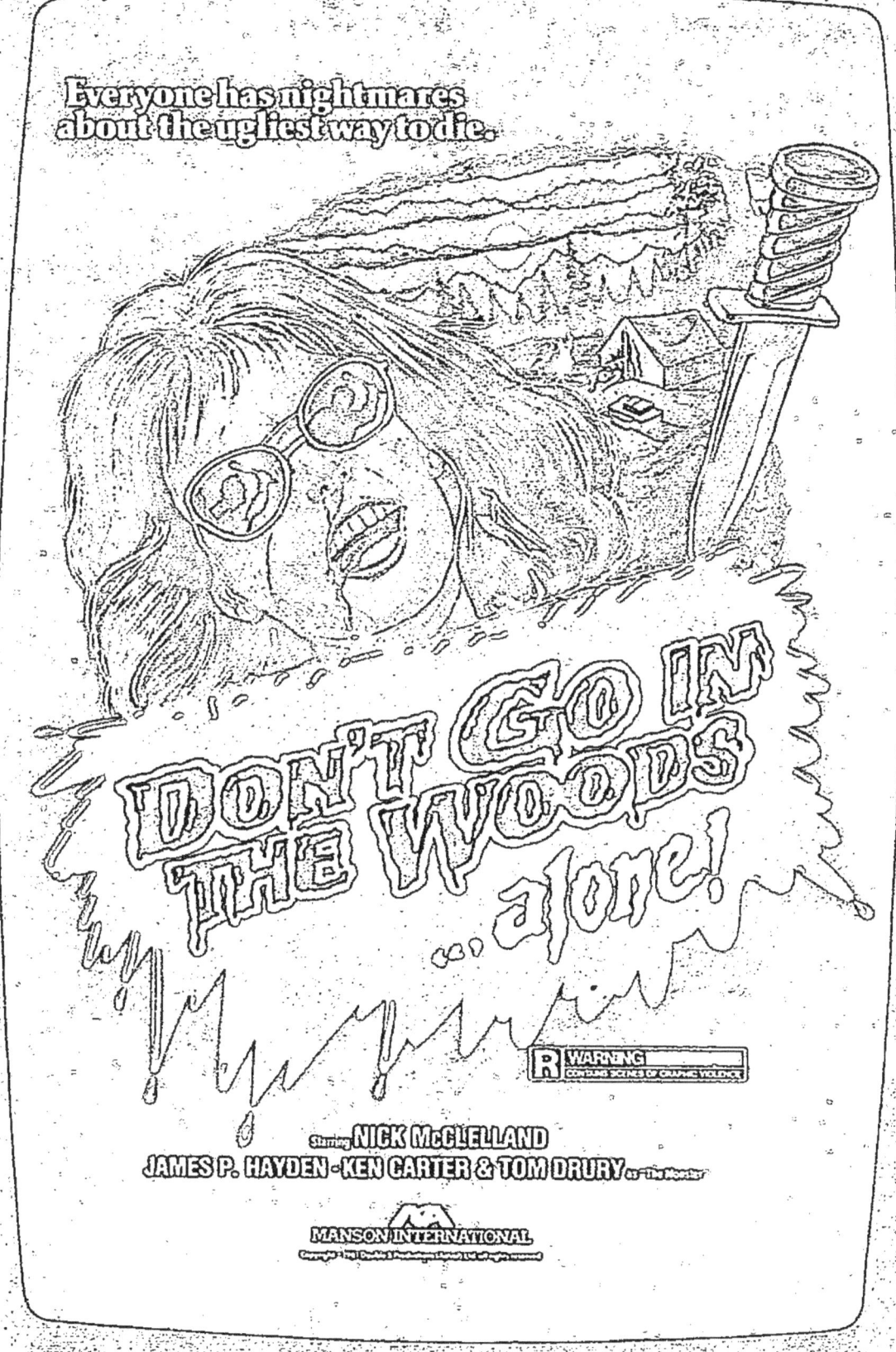

Something is alive in the Funhouse!

THE FUNHOUSE

From The Director Who Brought You The
"Texas-Chain-Saw-Massacre"

ELIZABETH BERRIDGE COOPER HUCKABEE MILES CHAPIN SYLVIA MILES
WILLIAM FINLEY KEVIN CONWAY as the Barker in THE FUNHOUSE
Written by LARRY BLOCK Directed by TOBE HOOPER
Produced by DEREK POWER and STEVEN BERNHARDT
Executive Producers MACE NEUFELD and MARK LESTER

A UNIVERSAL RELEASE READ THE JOVE BOOK
Copyright ©1981 by Universal City Studios, Inc.

RESTRICTED
UNDER 17 REQUIRES ACCOMPANYING
PARENT OR ADULT GUARDIAN

810070
"THE FUNHOUSE"

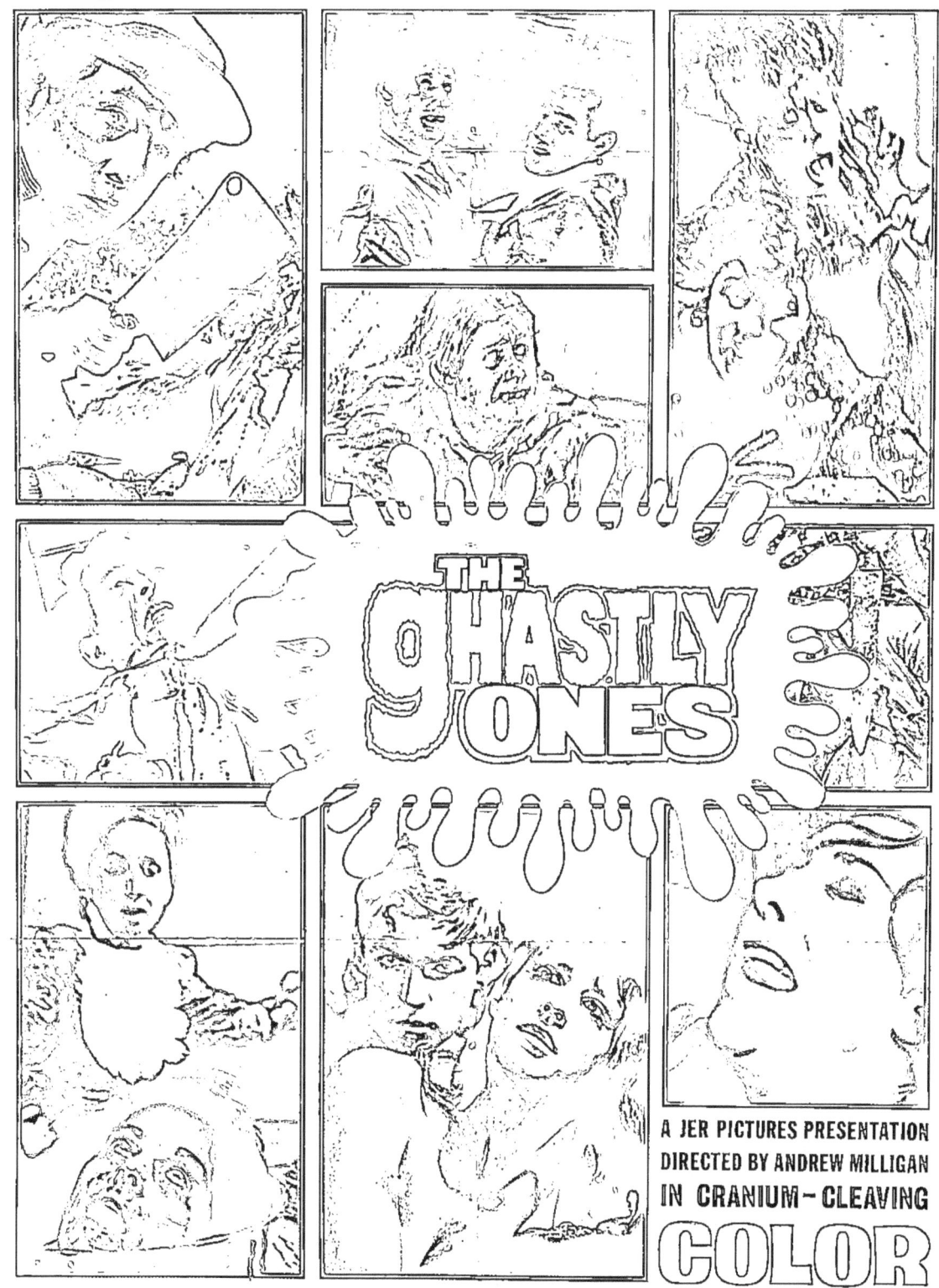

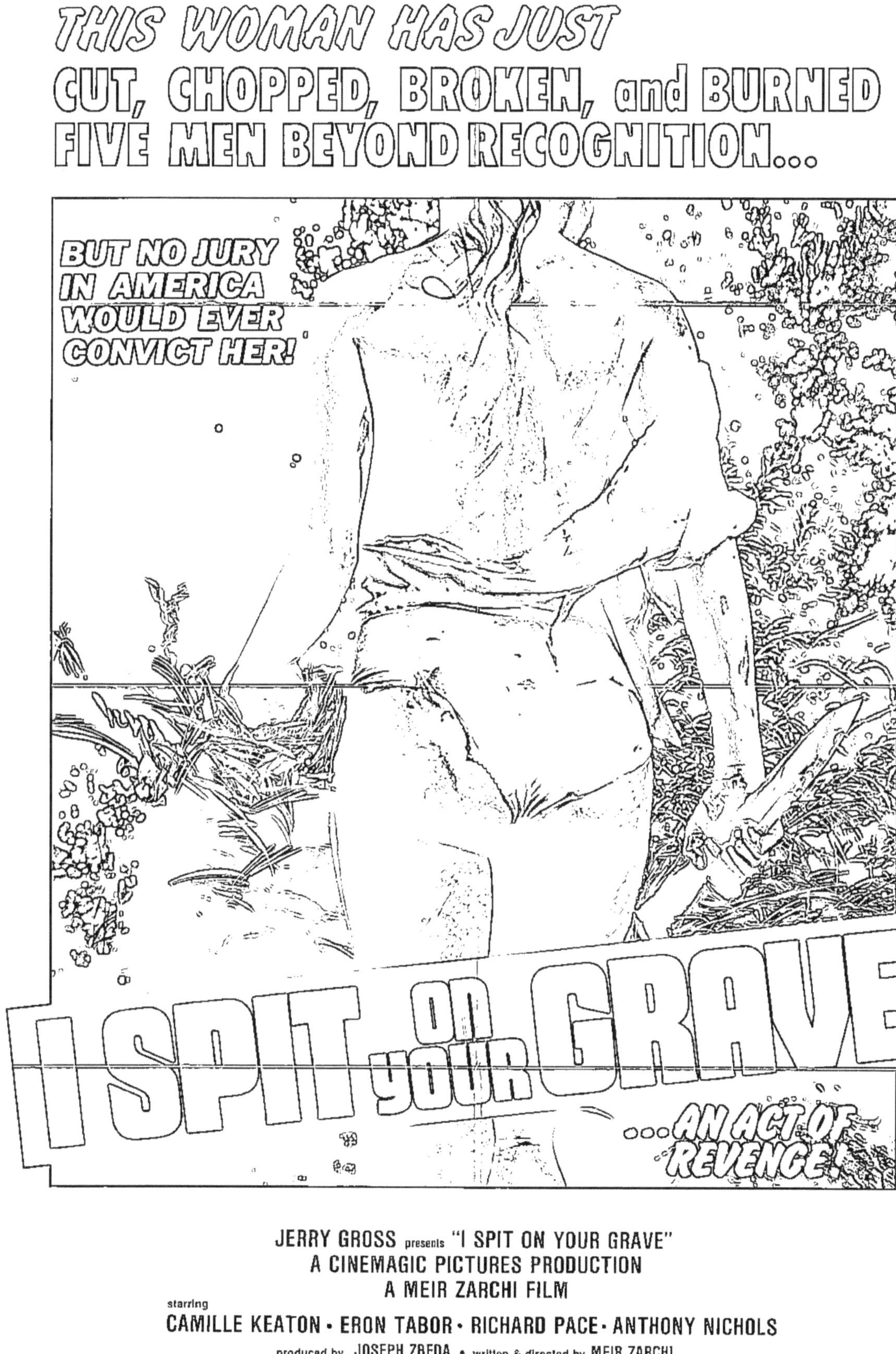

THIS WOMAN HAS JUST CUT, CHOPPED, BROKEN, and BURNED FIVE MEN BEYOND RECOGNITION...

BUT NO JURY IN AMERICA WOULD EVER CONVICT HER!

I SPIT ON YOUR GRAVE

...AN ACT OF REVENGE!

JERRY GROSS presents "I SPIT ON YOUR GRAVE"
A CINEMAGIC PICTURES PRODUCTION
A MEIR ZARCHI FILM

starring
CAMILLE KEATON • ERON TABOR • RICHARD PACE • ANTHONY NICHOLS
produced by JOSEPH ZBEDA • written & directed by MEIR ZARCHI
DISTRIBUTED BY THE JERRY GROSS ORGANIZATION   Color By METROCOLOR ®

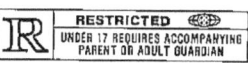

RESTRICTED
UNDER 17 REQUIRES ACCOMPANYING
PARENT OR ADULT GUARDIAN

It rests on 13 acres of earth over the very center of hell..!

MARI, SEVENTEEN, IS DYING.

EVEN FOR HER THE WORST IS YET TO COME!

SHE LIVED IN THE

LAST HOUSE ON THE LEFT

TO AVOID FAINTING KEEP REPEATING, IT'S ONLY A MOVIE ..ONLY A MOVIE ..ONLY A MOVIE ..ONLY A MOVIE ..ONLY A MOVIE ..ONLY A MOVIE ..ONLY A MOVIE

SEAN S. CUNNINGHAM FILMS LTD. Presents "THE LAST HOUSE ON THE LEFT"
Starring: DAVID HESS o LUCY GRANTHAM o SANDRA CASSEL o MARC SHEFFLER
o and introducing ADA WASHINGTON o Produced by SEAN S. CUNNINGHAM
Written and Directed by WES CRAVEN o COLOR BY MOVIELAB [R] RESTRICTED
Under 17 requires accompanying
Parent or Adult Guardian

WHEN THERE'S NO MORE ROOM IN HELL... THE DEAD WILL WALK THE EARTH!

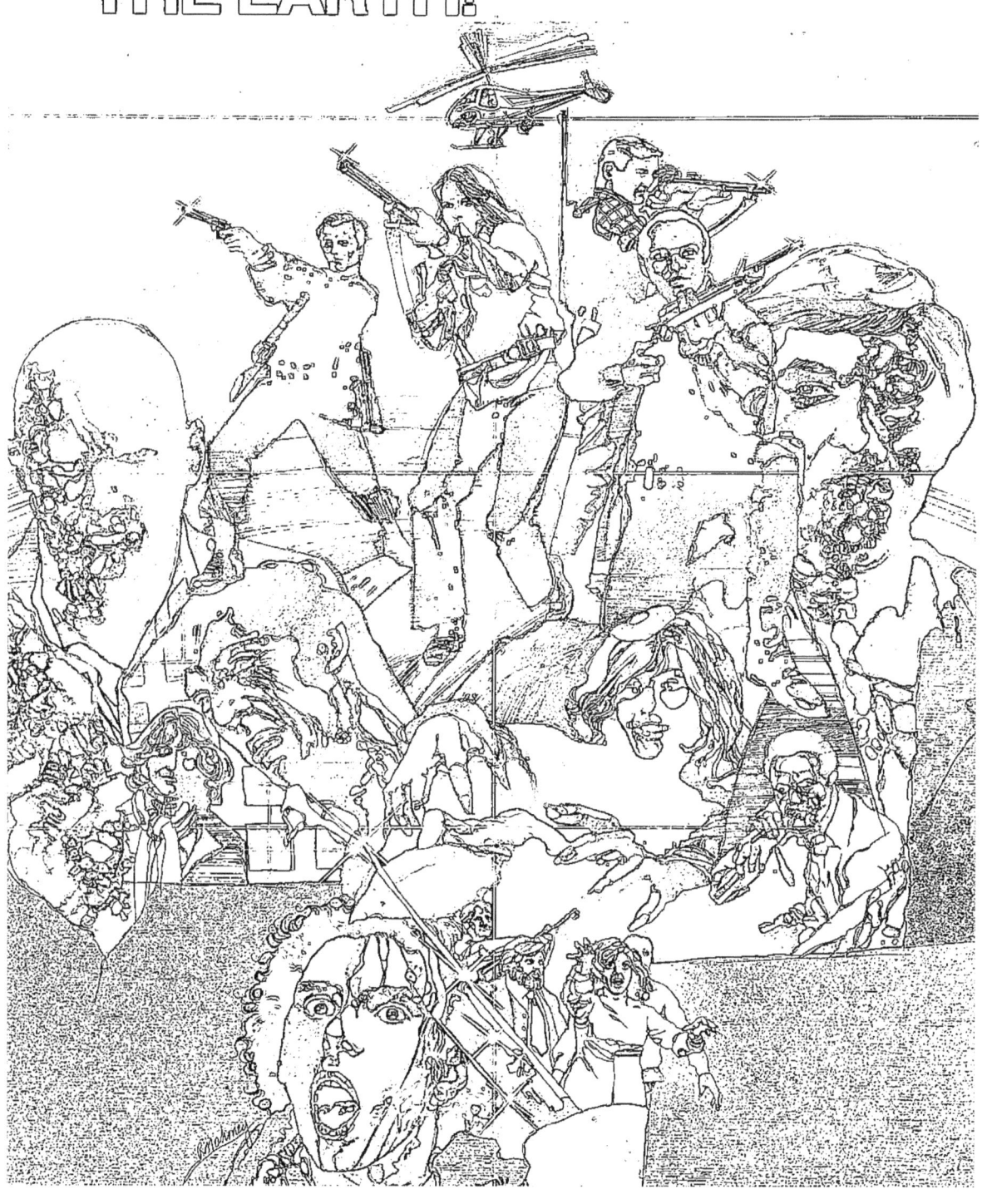

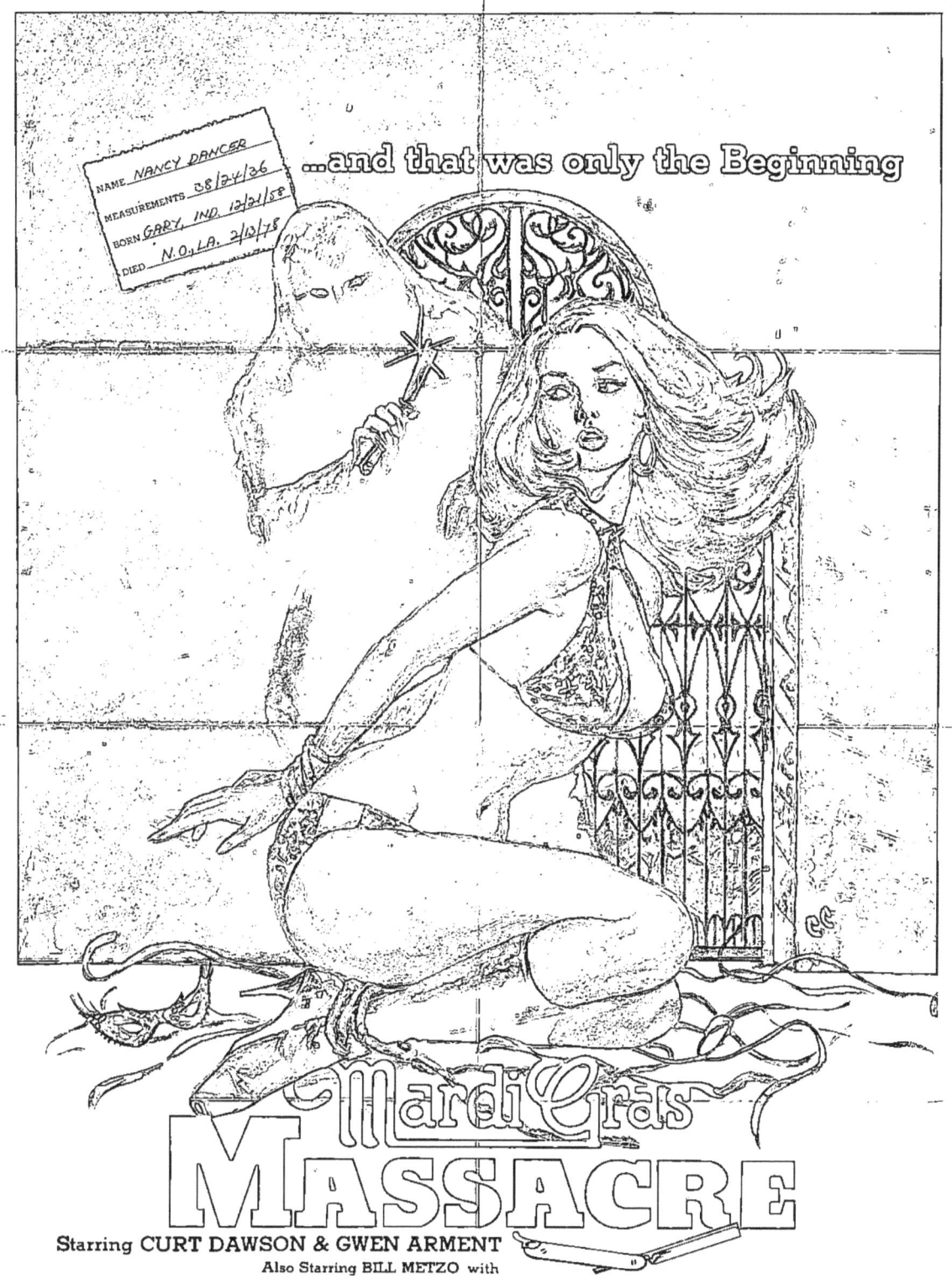

...and that was only the Beginning

NAME *NANCY DANCER*
MEASUREMENTS 38/24/36
BORN *GARY, IND.* 12/21/58
DIED *N.O., LA.* 2/13/78

Mardi Gras MASSACRE

Starring CURT DAWSON & GWEN ARMENT

Also Starring BILL METZO with
LAURA MISCH o CATHRYN LACEY o NANCY DANCER o BUTCH BENIT o WAYNE MACK and RONALD TANET
Assistant Producer JOHN STIMAC, Jr. o Cinematography by JACK Mc GOWAN o Produced and Directed by J. WEIS

IN COLOR
FROM OMNI CAPITAL RELEASING

WARNING o DUE TO SHOCKING SCENES OF EXTREME VIOLENCE
o WE RECOMMEND NO ONE UNDER 17 BE ADMITTED.

American cannibale

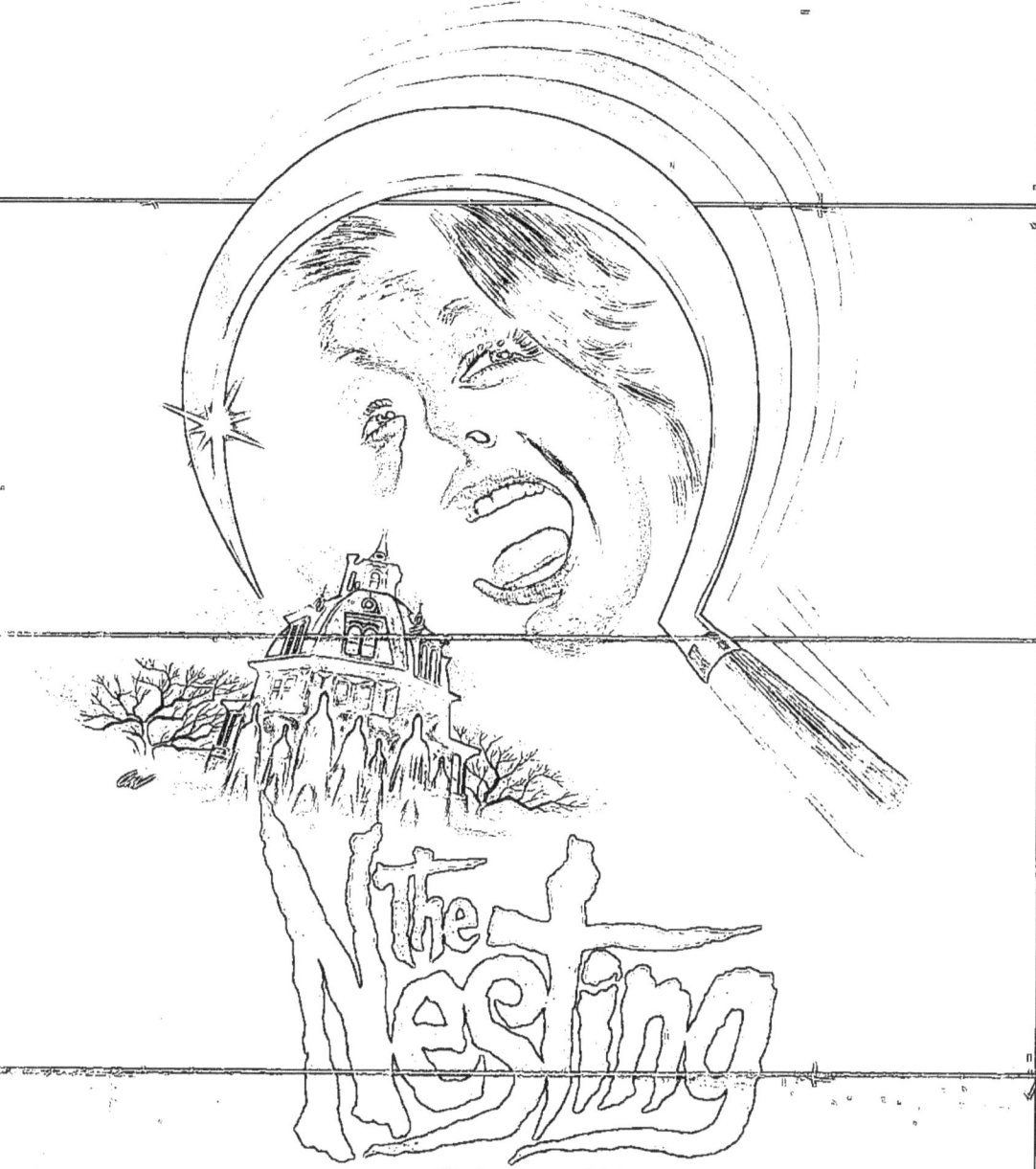

The terror that hides inside your mind.

The Nesting

a film by Armand Weston

Starring ROBIN GROVES with CHRISTOPHER LOOMIS and MICHAEL DAVID LALLY
and JOHN CARRADINE as the Colonel and GLORIA GRAHAME as Florinda
Executive Producers Sam Lake and Robert Sumner ○ Associate Producer Don Walters
Music by Jack Malken and Kim Scholes
Screenplay by Daria Price and Armand Weston ○ Produced and Directed by Armand Weston

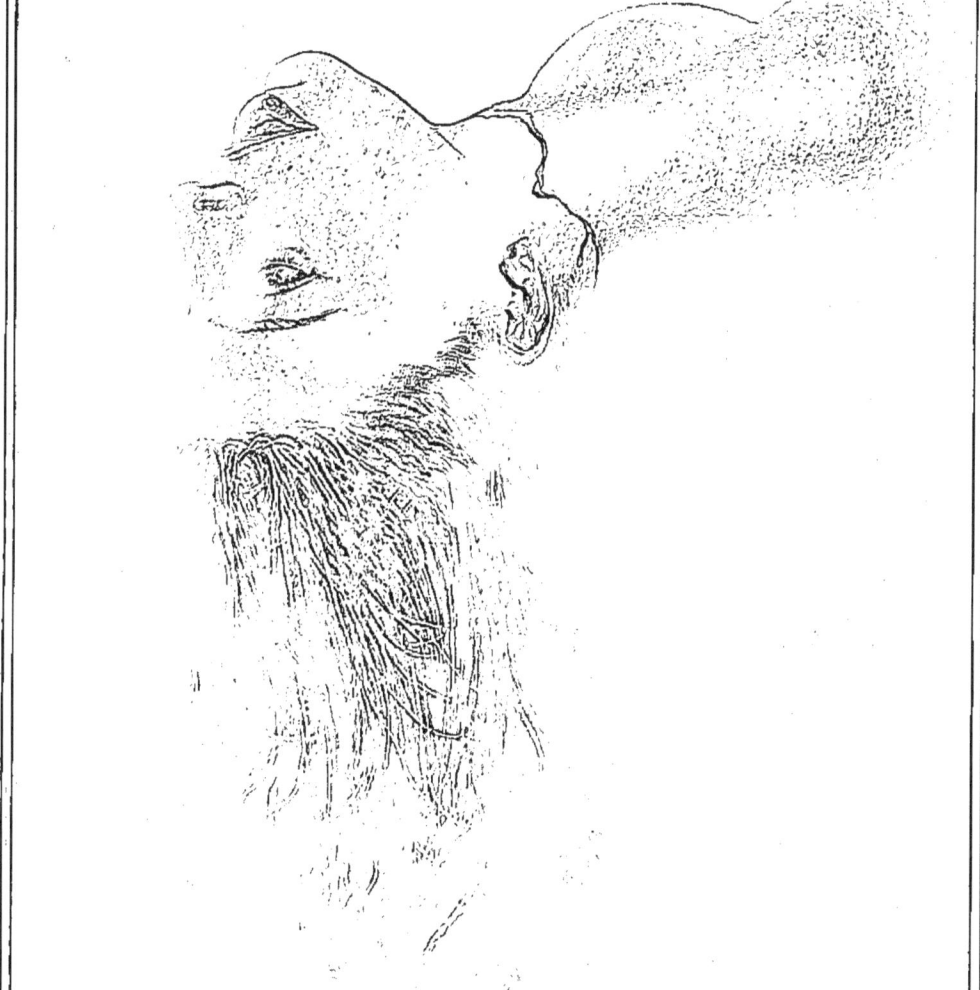

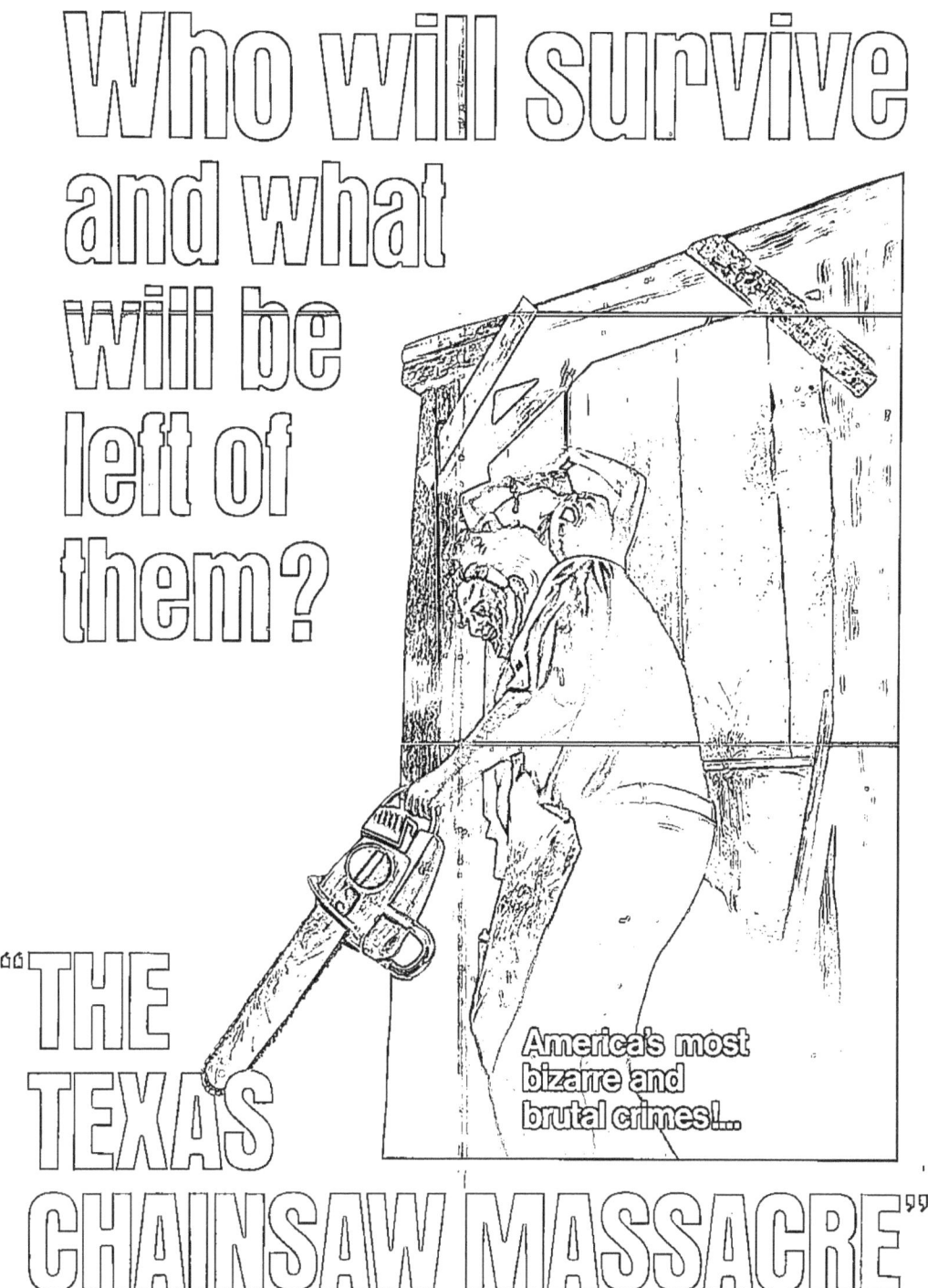

Who will survive and what will be left of them?

America's most bizarre and brutal crimes!...

"THE TEXAS CHAINSAW MASSACRE"

What happened is true. Now the motion picture that's just as real.

THE TEXAS CHAIN SAW MASSACRE · A Film by TOBE HOOPER · Starring MARILYN BURNS, PAUL A. PARTAIN, EDWIN NEAL, JIM SIEDOW and GUNNAR HANSEN as "Leatherface" · Production Manager, RONALD BOZMAN · Music Score by TOBE HOOPER and WAYNE BELL · Music Performed by ARKEY BLUE, ROGER BARTLETT & FRIENDS, TIMBERLINE ROSE, LOS CYCLONES · Story & Screenplay by KIM HENKEL and TOBE HOOPER · Producer/Director, TOBE HOOPER · COLOR · A BRYANSTON PICTURES RELEASE.

R RESTRICTED

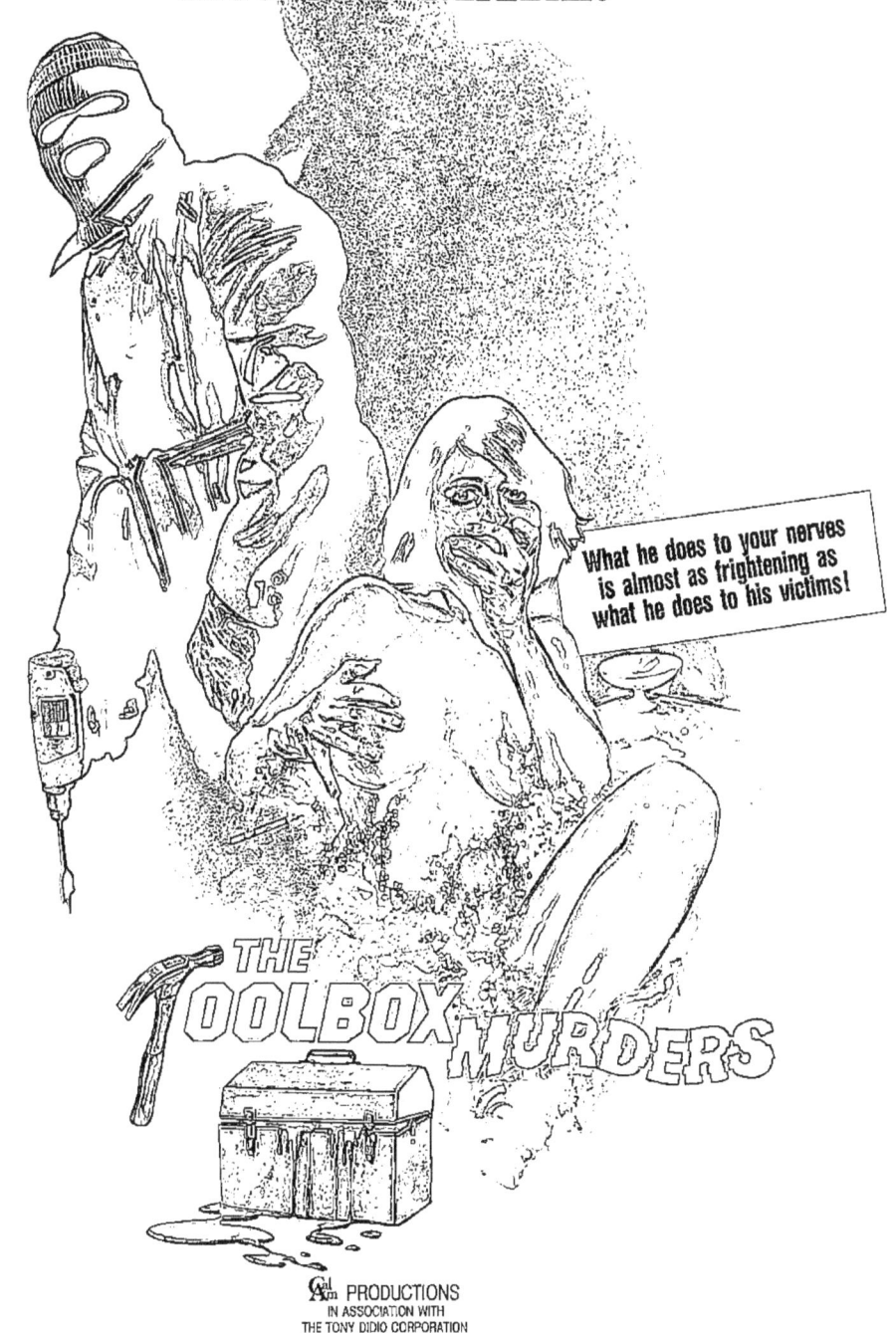

BIT BY BIT...BY BIT HE CARVED A NIGHTMARE!

What he does to your nerves is almost as frightening as what he does to his victims!

THE TOOLBOX MURDERS

Cal-Am PRODUCTIONS
IN ASSOCIATION WITH
THE TONY DIDIO CORPORATION
PRESENTS

"THE TOOLBOX MURDERS" Starring CAMERON MITCHELL

PAMELYN FERDIN and WESLEY EURE · Produced by TONY DIDIO · Directed by DENNIS DONNELLY

Associate Producers
KENNETH A. YATES and JACK KINDBERG · ROBERT EASTER and ANN N. KINDBERG
Story and Screenplay by

Music Composed and Conducted by GEORGE DEATON · Color Prints by CFI

RESTRICTED
UNDER 17 REQUIRES ACCOMPANYING
PARENT OR ADULT GUARDIAN

A Cal-Am Artists Release
© 1978 Cal-Am Productions, Inc.

790035

"THE TOOLBOX MURDERS"

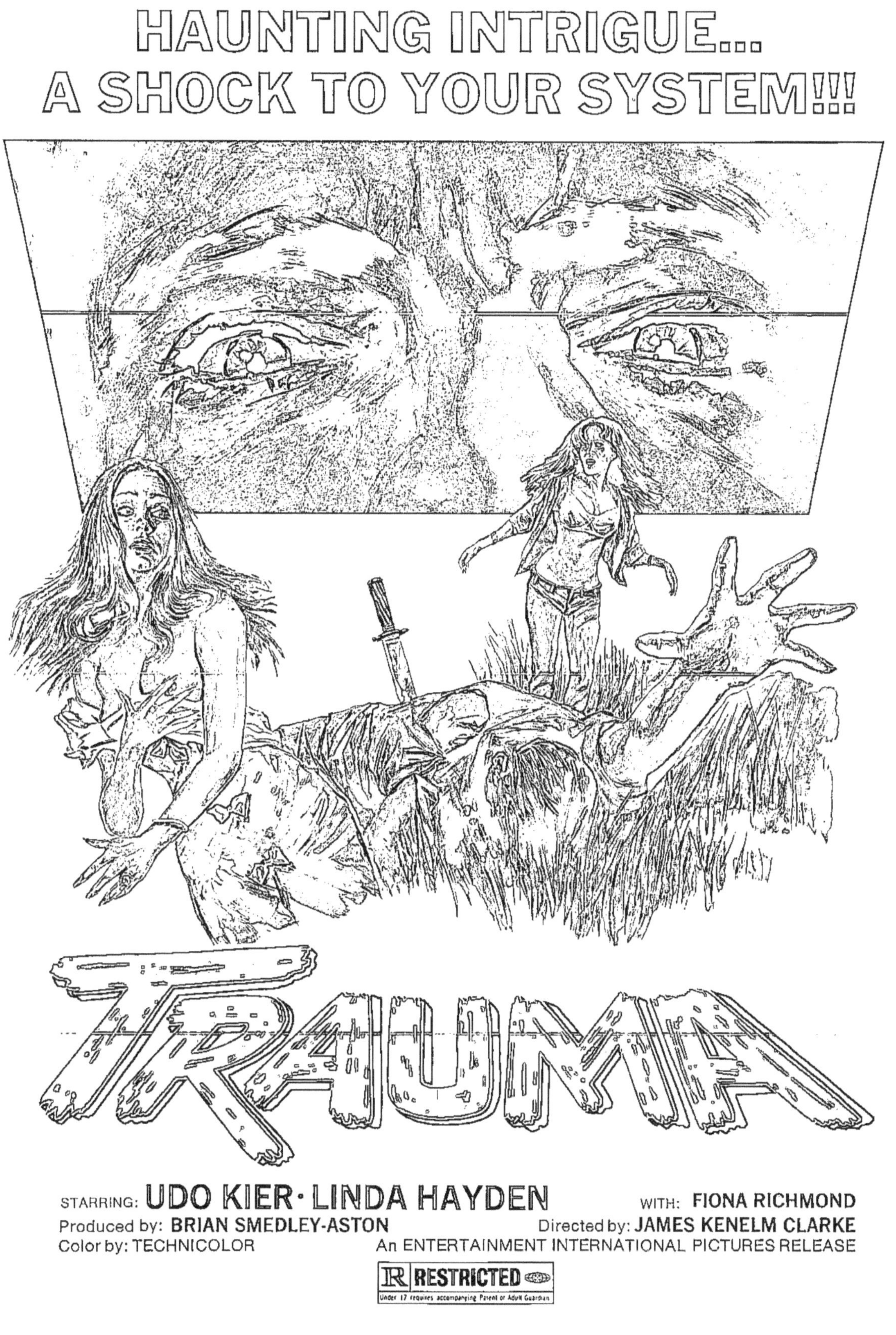

HAUNTING INTRIGUE...
A SHOCK TO YOUR SYSTEM!!!

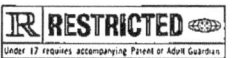

TRAUMA

STARRING: **UDO KIER · LINDA HAYDEN** WITH: **FIONA RICHMOND**

Produced by: **BRIAN SMEDLEY-ASTON** Directed by: **JAMES KENELM CLARKE**

Color by: TECHNICOLOR An ENTERTAINMENT INTERNATIONAL PICTURES RELEASE

R **RESTRICTED**
Under 17 requires accompanying Parent or Adult Guardian

"TRAUMA" 76/230

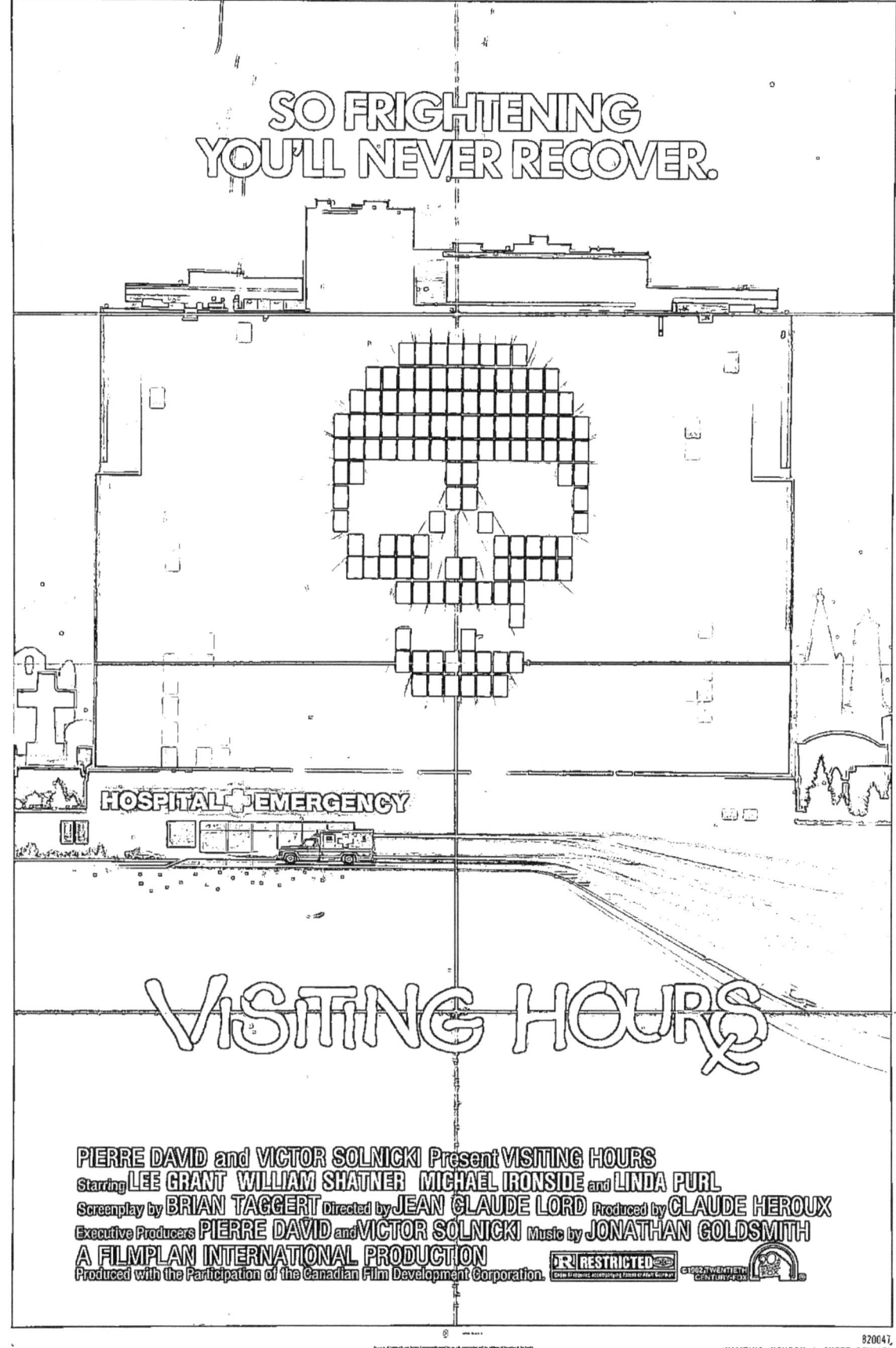

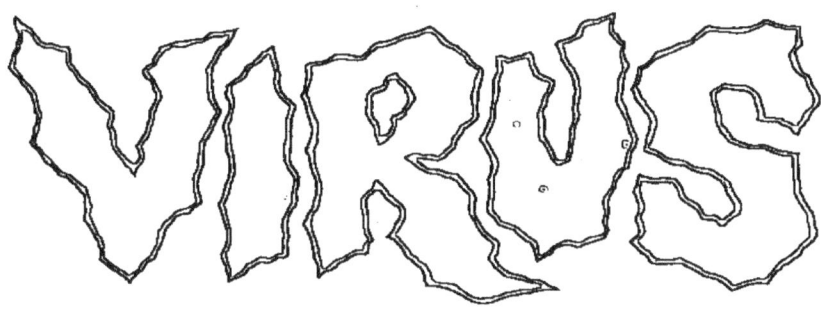

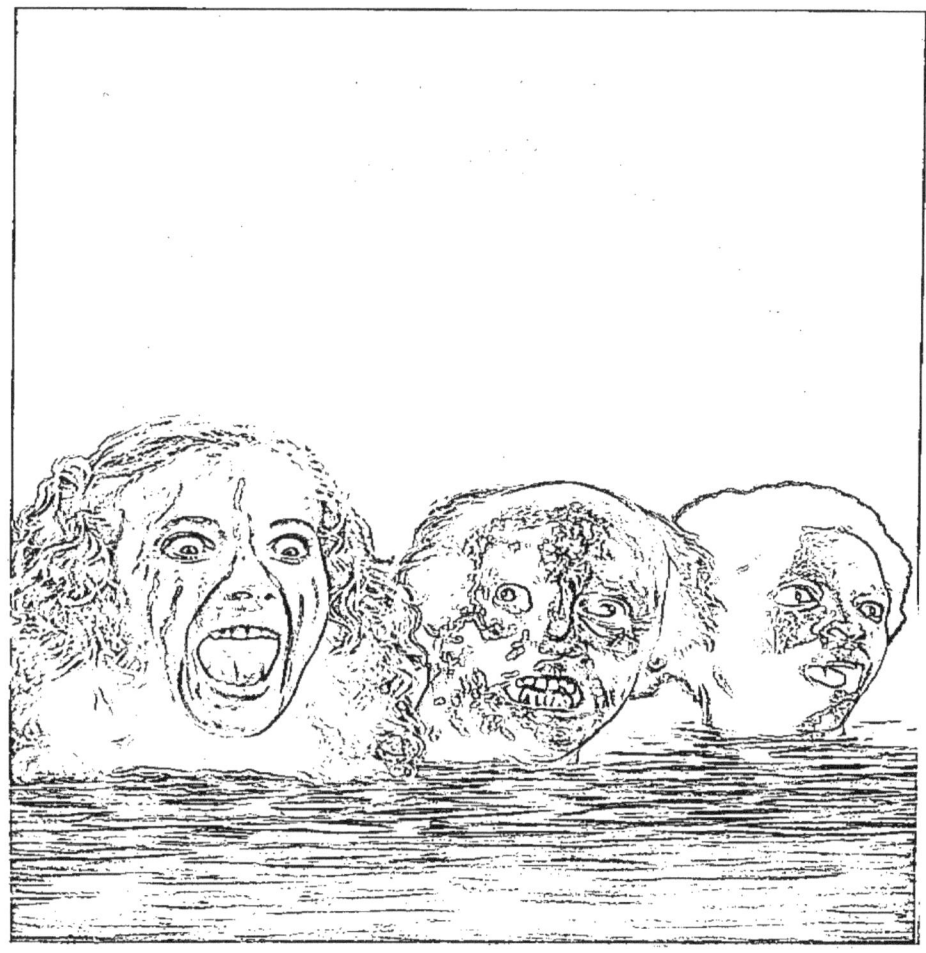

MARGI EVELYN NEWTON · FRANK GARFEELD · SELAN KARAY · ROBERT O'NEIL
GABY RENOM · LUIS FONOLL · Musiche dei "GOBLIN" a cura di G. DELL'ORSO | EDIZIONI MUSICALI GRANDI FIRME DELLA CANZONE
Regia di VINCENT DAWN Una coproduzione : BEATRICE FILM s.r.l. ROMA · FILMS DARA · BARCELLONA | United Artists Europa Inc. A Transamerica Company

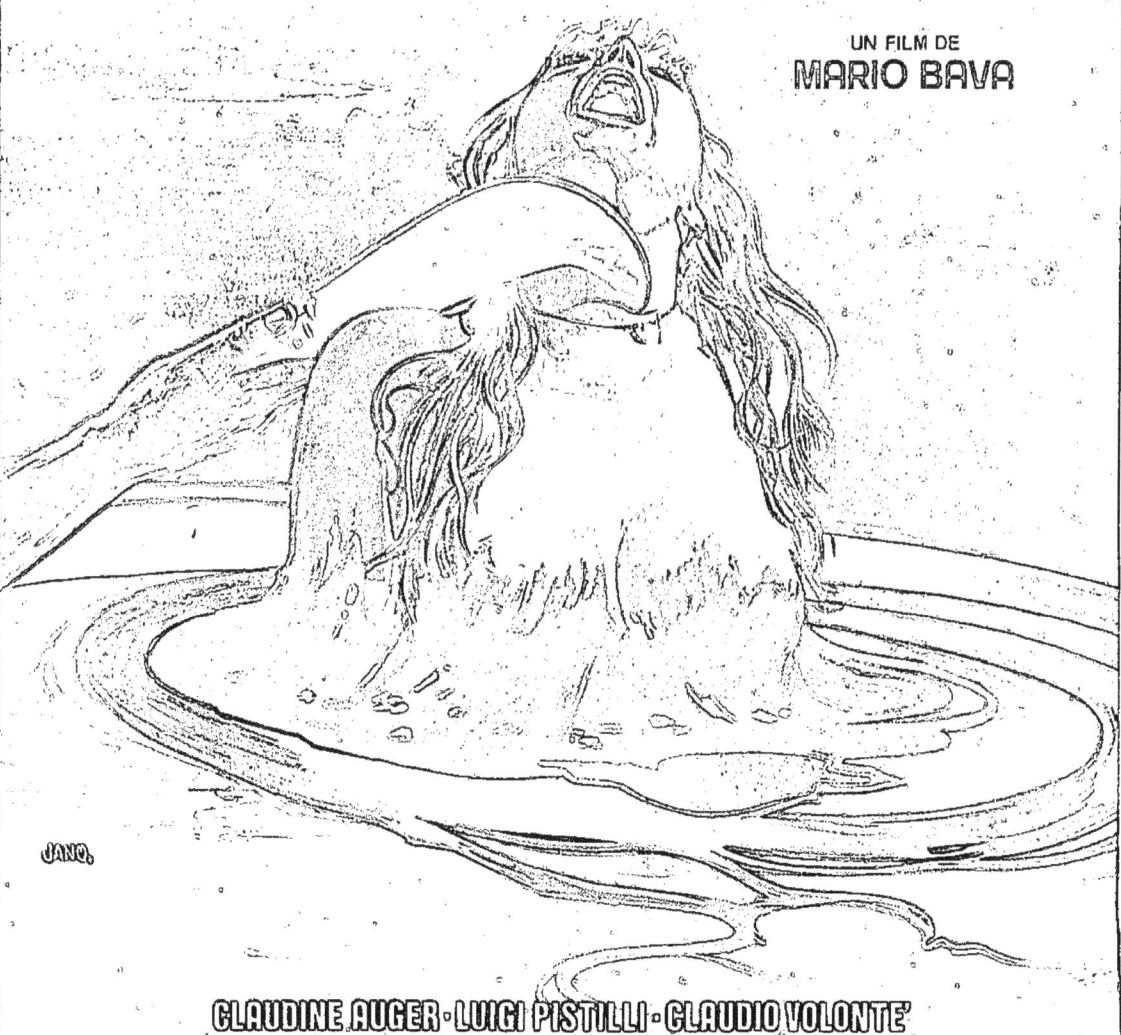

INTERNATIONAL FILMS
DISTRIBUTION, S.A.

BAHIA DE SANGRE

UN FILM DE
MARIO BAVA

JANO.

CLAUDINE AUGER · LUIGI PISTILLI · CLAUDIO VOLONTE'

LAURA BETTI · LEOPOLDO TRIESTE · BRIGITTE SKAY

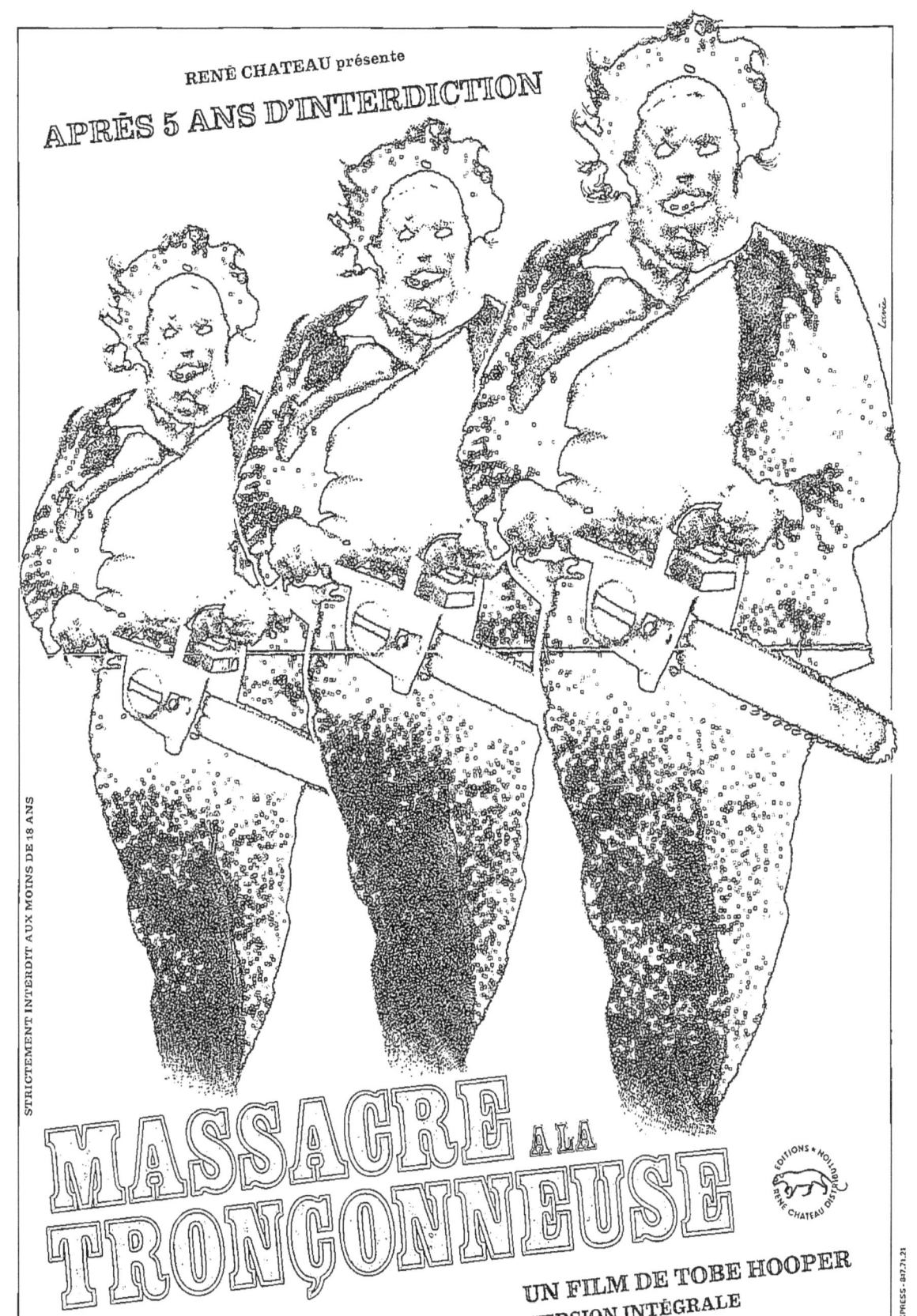

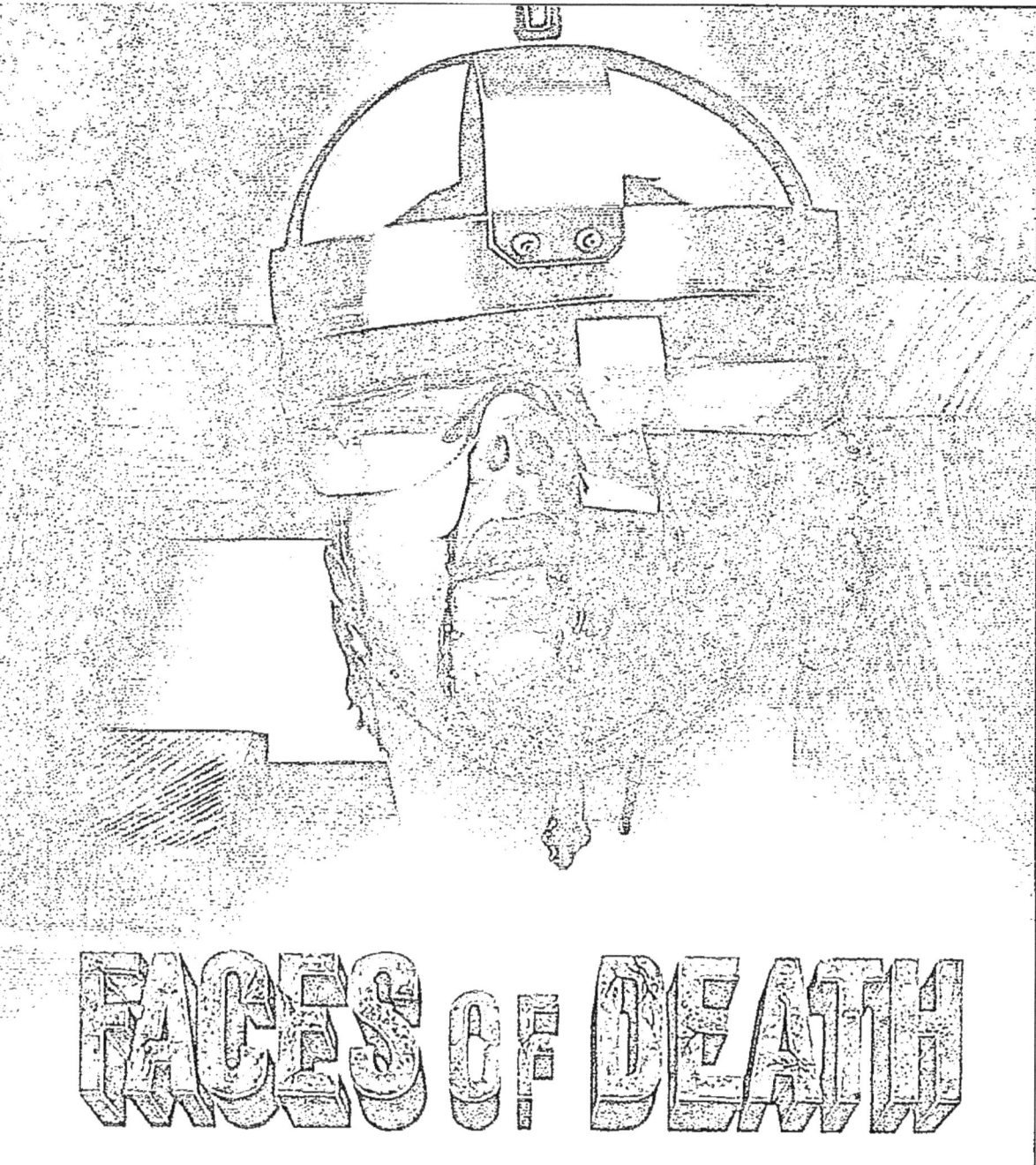

Prepare yourself for the ultimate experience.
This video cassette will change your attitude
to life.

Executive Producer: William B. James
Producer: Rosilyn T. Scott
Director: Conan Le Cilaire

TRUE LIFE HORROR
Colour - AVP 601

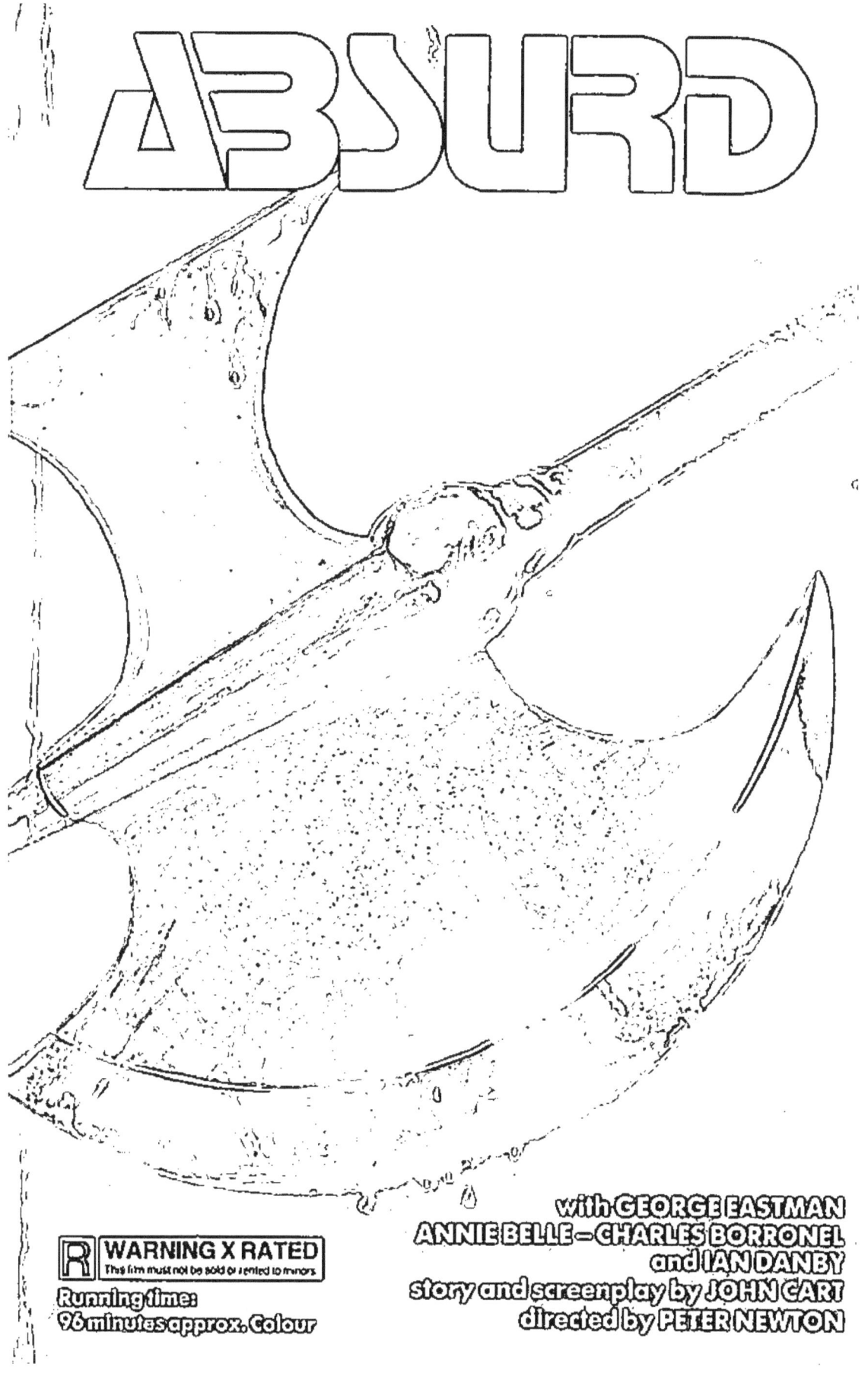

ABSURD

with GEORGE EASTMAN
ANNIE BELLE – CHARLES BORRONEL
and IAN DANBY
story and screenplay by JOHN CART
directed by PETER NEWTON

R | **WARNING X RATED**
This film must not be sold or rented to minors.

Running time:
96 minutes approx. Colour

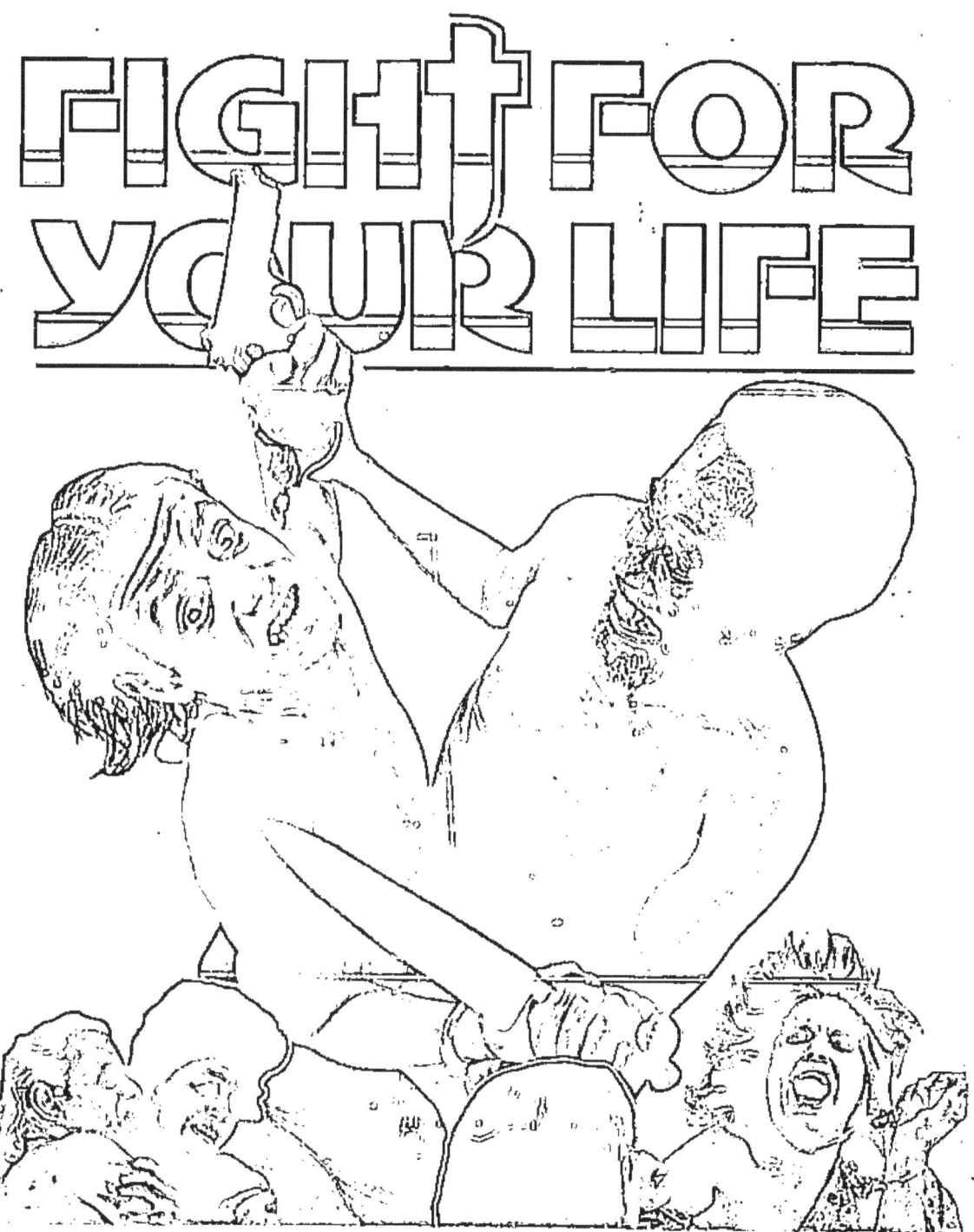

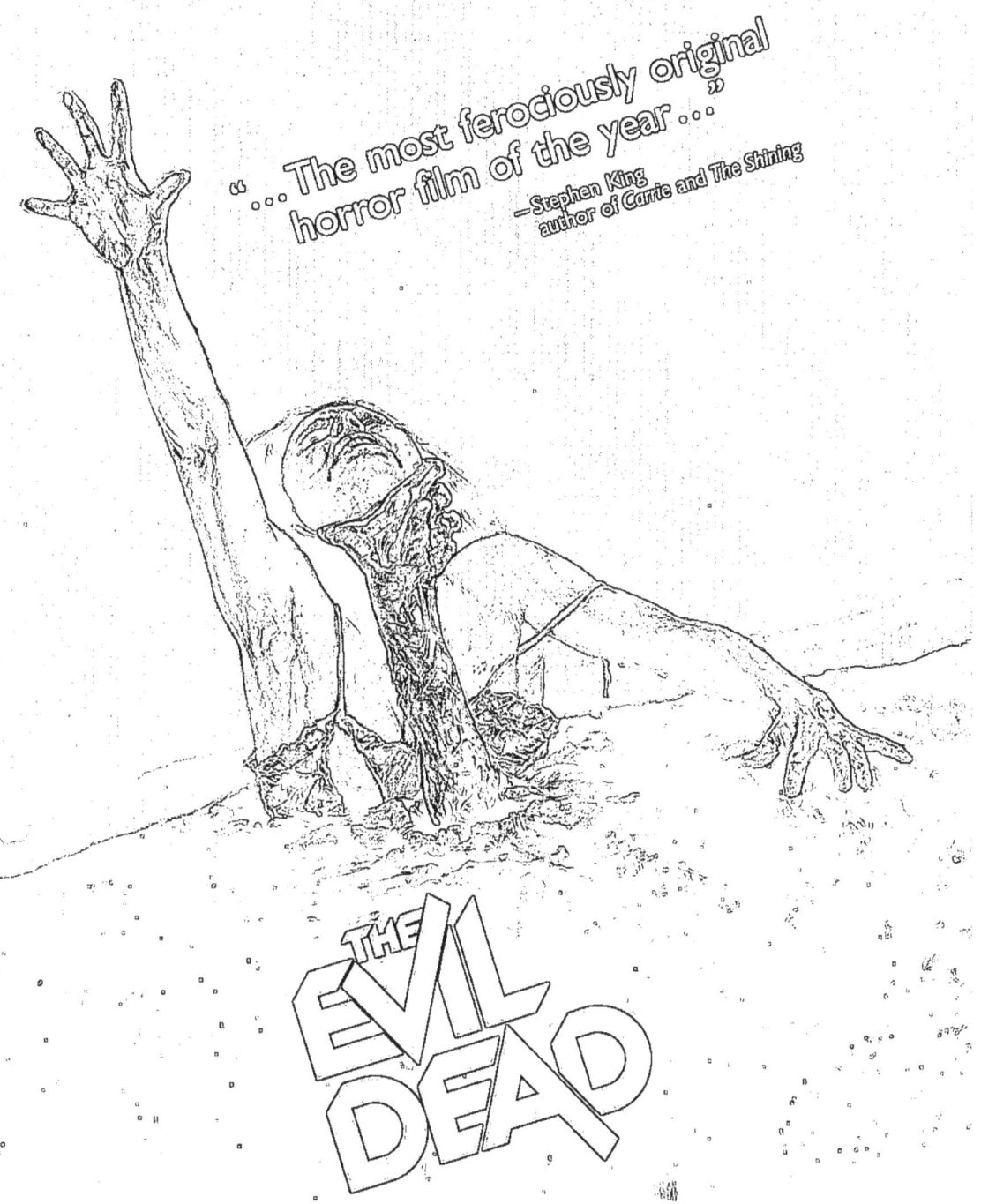

" ... The most ferociously original horror film of the year ... "

—Stephen King
author of *Carrie* and *The Shining*

THE EVIL DEAD

Starring BRUCE CAMPBELL ELLEN SANDWEISS HAL DELRICH BETSY BAKER SARAH YORK
Make-up Effects by TOM SULLIVAN Photographic Effects by BART PIERCE Photography by TIM PHILO
Music by JOE LoDUCA Produced by ROBERT G. TAPERT Written and Directed by SAM RAIMI
Color by TECHNICOLOR® Renaissance Pictures Ltd. From NEW LINE CINEMA All Rights Reserved

©New Line Cinema Corp. MCMLXXXII

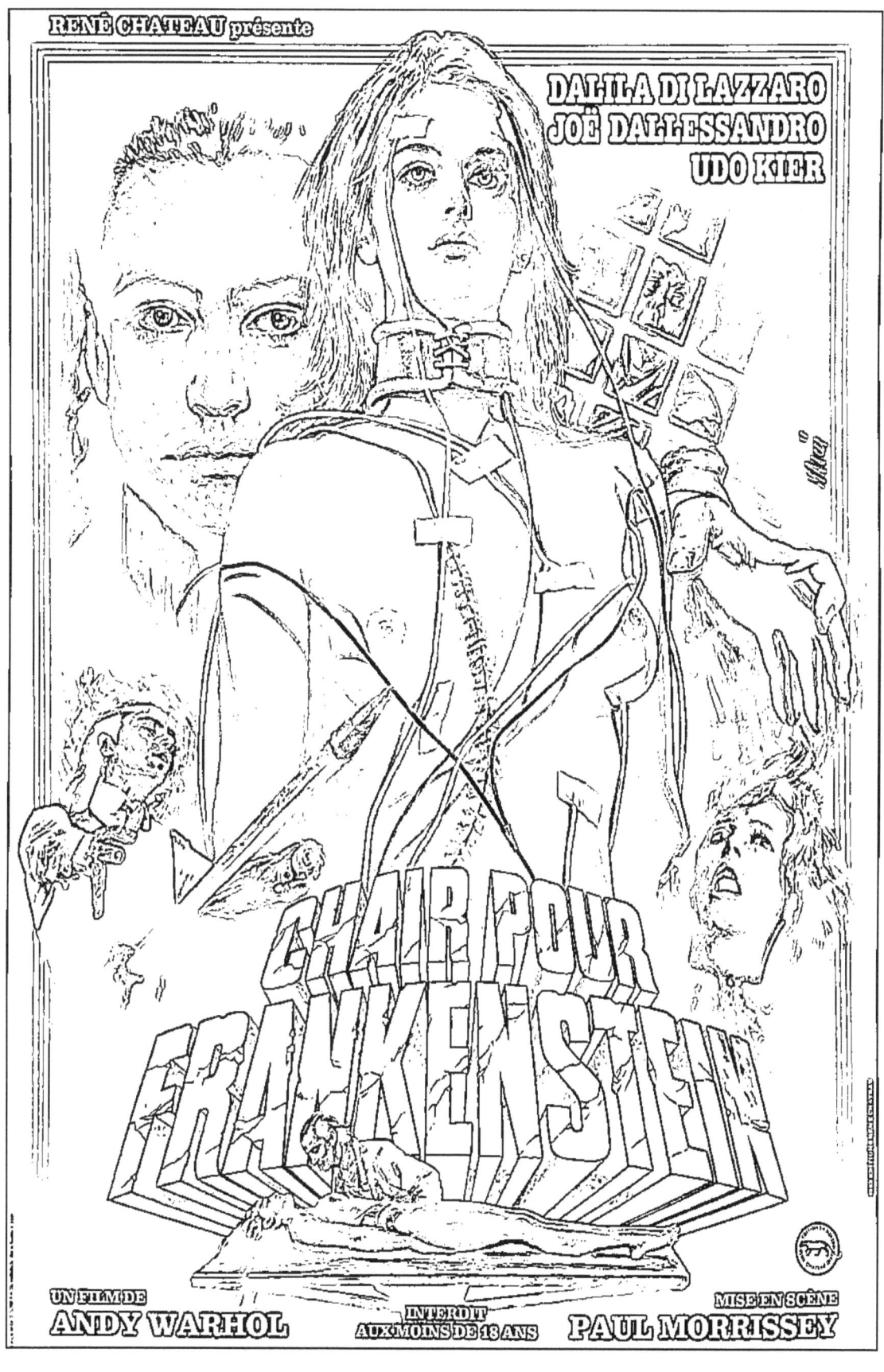

www.ingramcontent.com/pod-product-compliance
Lightning Source LLC
Chambersburg PA
CBHW080711190526
45169CB00006B/2333